VATICAN II TODAY

VATICAN II TODAY
Calling Catholics to Holiness and Service

EDITED BY
JUDY BALL
AND
JOAN MCKAMEY

ST. ANTHONY MESSENGER PRESS
Cincinnati, Ohio

Imprimatur: Carl K. Moeddel, Vicar General and Auxiliary Bishop, Archdiocese of Cincinnati, December 16, 2003—November 29, 2004

The *imprimatur* is a declaration that a book or pamphlet is considered to be free from doctrinal or moral error. It is not implied that those who have granted the *imprimatur* agree with the contents, opinions or statements expressed.

Cover and book design by Mark Sullivan

Library of Congress Cataloging-in-Publication Data

Vatican II today : called to holiness and service / edited by Judy Ball.
    p. cm.
    ISBN 0-86716-670-3 (pbk. : alk. paper) 1. Vatican Council (2nd : 1962-1965) I. Title: Vatican 2 today. II. Title: Vatican Two today. III. Ball, Judy.

BX8301962 .V328 2005
262'.52—dc22

                                                                2005015764

0-86716-670-3

Published by St. Anthony Messenger Press
28 W. Liberty St.
Cincinnati, OH 45202
www.AmericanCatholic.org

Printed in the United States of America
Printed on acid-free paper

05 06 07 08 09 5 4 3 2 1

CONTENTS

CHAPTER ONE

Road Map for the Future: Teachings of Vatican II

JACK WINTZ, O.F.M., AND JOHN FEISTER

Vatican II (1962–1965) was one of the great moments in the history of our church. It marked a time when the church took a look at where it was and where the world was—and sought to close the gap. The Council wasn't a sudden event; years of changes in the world and years of study among church leaders and theologians brought us all to that great moment.

> The momentum behind the church's ongoing renewal is found in the teachings of Vatican II. It is found in a church re-centered on the Gospels and the Eucharist and in constant dialogue with the world.

Although Pope John XXIII (1958–1963) is rightly given credit for initiating the Second Vatican Council, the preparations for a council had been discussed for many years. But it was Pope John, a student of church history with firsthand experience of the joys and troubles of the world, who brought the spirit of informed openness that so shaped Vatican II. And of course it is to the credit of his successor, Paul VI (1963–1978), that the Council moved forward following John's death.

It was the timing of that Council—at the dawn of satellite communications—that suddenly put the church in touch with more of the world. Evangelizing possibilities were now greater than ever; but now, too, the world could look in on the church and challenge it.

Years later, we are still challenged by the work of the Council Fathers, the 2,860 bishops who drafted the Council's sixteen documents. We've been through periods of experimentation, reimagining who we are as church. Some have decried the changes as too much, too fast; others have complained that the church isn't changing fast enough.

It has been said that a church council's vision is not realized until the third generation—two generations after those who held the Council. Our church today includes adults of this third

1

generation. Those who were at the Council or remember it are fewer and fewer. Those who were children during the Council are split between those who experienced strong church formation and those whose faith formation was probably, at least initially, lacking in many basics. Many of those born in the mid-1960s and later struggle today to understand their faith in depth.

The momentum behind the church's ongoing renewal is found in the teachings of Vatican II. It is found in a church that is re-centered on the Gospels and the Eucharist and in constant dialogue with the world. Pope John Paul II said it best a few years ago: "The best preparation for the new millennium can only be expressed by a renewed commitment *to apply*, as faithfully as possible, the teachings of Vatican II to the life of every individual and of the whole church" (*The Coming Third Millennium*, 20).

This book will look at the principal documents of the Council and give a report, of sorts, on our progress as Catholics. The Council documents provide a road map for our future; this book will explore our progress along that route. We begin by taking a broad look at some of the major trends that the Council initiated.

MINISTRY TRANSFORMATION

It's common today to see laypeople assisting at Mass as eucharistic ministers. These and other lay liturgical ministers—ushers, greeters, lectors and music ministers—are visible reminders of the wide variety of laypeople who minister within the church. Some serve as catechists or youth ministers, others as hospital chaplains, bereavement ministers, administrators of priestless parishes and outreach workers.

Behind this burgeoning lay involvement in ministry is the reality that more Catholics are embracing their baptismal call to ministry or service to the Catholic community and, indeed, to the world at large.

At the same time that the role of the laity is growing, we are experiencing a decline in the number of ordained ministers. The Holy Spirit is clearly leading us to a more inclusive model of church in which we recognize the need for both lay and ordained ministers to make the work of the church complete.

Women are among those becoming more engaged in church ministry today, though many believe that their potential has not been fully realized. What full ministry for women should mean is a sensitive question requiring further discernment. Those awaiting greater acknowledgment in the church also include ethnic minorities, Catholics with disabilities and many others whose gifts have not yet been fully respected or utilized.

THEN AND NOW
Vatican I (1869–1870)

Vatican I is best summed up in two words: papal infallibility. Initially, Pope Pius IX wanted the Council to address various issues of the day such as church-state relations, the lifestyle and morals of the clergy and the need for a universal catechism. But, from the start, the primacy and infallibility of the pope became the primary focus for the eight hundred churchmen who gathered at the first council to be held in St. Peter's Basilica.

Up to 80 percent of them were "infallibilists" who supported the notion that the pope is incapable of error when speaking officially and in very specific circumstances on matters of faith and morals. Others either opposed the idea outright or objected to the definition of the term. When the final vote came, however, it was 433 to 2. Immediately after, the two dissenting bishops joined the others in accepting the idea that the Holy Father exercises infallibility on specific occasions on behalf of and in communion with the church. Ultimately, all bishops in the world gave their adherence.

Vatican I was suddenly suspended when Rome was invaded; sessions never resumed. Though the spiritual power of the papacy was strengthened at Vatican I, it left the relationship between the Holy Father and bishops unsettled and unclear.

DYNAMIC LITURGIES

The liturgical renewal that swept through the church after Vatican II brought new life to the celebration of the Eucharist and other sacraments. New sacramental rites and the use of local languages encourage more full and active participation.

Before Vatican II, the priest celebrated Mass in Latin with his back to the people, making the action of the Mass seem far away. It was easy for the faithful to fall into the role of spectators. Now the assembly is more actively engaged, helping us to experience "all of us" celebrating the Eucharist with the priest. Vatican II's *Constitution on the Sacred Liturgy* urges "full, conscious and active participation in liturgical celebrations" (14).

The church now stresses the communal dimension of all the sacraments, seeing them as "community events," not private rituals. The RCIA (*Rite of Christian Initiation of Adults*) is a dramatic sign of this communal approach to the sacraments.

Before the RCIA was reestablished, the typical approach to adult baptism was isolated from the parish community. Preparation often consisted of around six weeks of private instruction followed by baptism on a Sunday afternoon, attended by a small cluster of relatives or friends.

Today, the RCIA process lasts a year or more and involves sponsors, catechists and, indeed, the whole parish. The Sacraments of Initiation—baptism, confirmation and Eucharist—are celebrated within the context of community at the Easter Vigil. This spirit of communal involvement is also reflected in other sacraments.

NEW INTEREST IN SCRIPTURE

More Catholics are reading the Bible today—with more solid understanding—than at any other time in church history.

Growing numbers of laypeople are attending theology schools, joining or even leading Bible study groups, and reading an array of solid articles or books on the subject. Priests and religious are no longer the only Scripture experts.

The church today encourages its members to make use of new methods of Scripture study and to cherish the Scriptures. Catholics are growing in their understanding of the Bible through the benefits of historical research, literary analysis and archaeological findings. Church documents wisely steer Catholics away from literal-minded approaches and from reading the Bible as if it were a science or history textbook.

Also of note is that, through the lectionary's three-year cycle, Catholics are now exposed to a wider variety of Scripture readings at Sunday Mass. The use of Scripture readings has been enhanced in other sacramental rites as well.

As Catholics are nourished by the life-giving word of God, they become better instruments of evangelization and of the world's transformation.

OUTREACH TO ALL HUMANITY

One of the most warmly received insights of Vatican II is that salvation is concerned not solely with saving souls but also with saving the whole person—body and soul. This holistic view is appealing because we naturally do not want to lose any genuine part of our human experience. Saint Irenaeus, often quoted at the time of the Second Vatican Council, captured this well: "The glory of God is the human person fully alive!"

Jesus' mission on this earth was not only to free the human heart from sin, but also to free men and women from disease, oppression and everything that hinders their development as humans created by God and destined for eternal life. When we profess our belief in the resurrection of the body, this integral salvation is implied.

In *The Church in the Modern World,* the bishops of Vatican II acknowledged the intimate bond between the church and all humanity. This great document begins: "The joys and hopes, the grief and anguish of the people of our time, especially those who are poor or afflicted, are the joys and hopes, the grief and anguish of the followers of Christ. Nothing that is genuinely human fails to find an echo in their hearts."

This conviction is evident in a new commitment to ecumenism as well as the acknowledgment of salvation outside of the Catholic church (*Dogmatic Constitution on the Church,* 15–16). In addition to his many heroic firsts in the ecumenical effort, Pope John Paul II powerfully expressed this attitude during his first visit to the United States in October 1979. His opening words were: "I want to greet all Americans without distinction. I want to tell everyone that the pope is your friend and a servant of your humanity."

Every authentic dimension of human existence is to be saved and brought to wholeness. As the pope's words suggest, we are to help all people come to their full humanity as men and women created in the image and likeness of God and redeemed by Christ.

GETTING PERSONAL

LADISLAS ORSY, S.J.

When Pope John XXIII announced in early 1959 his intention to call an ecumenical council, a young Jesuit priest named Ladislas Orsy was as surprised and puzzled as other church-watchers were. Where, he wondered, would such a council take the church, and what would its significance be? He waited for the answers at the Gregorian University, where he was teaching canon law.

Today, decades later, Father Orsy, now eighty-two, still has questions. "The further away we are from the Second Vatican Council, the more I am discovering its enormous significance and how much more we have to understand," he said. Just by calling a council and turning to the bishops for their insights and wisdom, Pope John reversed a trend toward centralized papal power that dated to the Council of Trent in the sixteenth century. Now canon law professor at Georgetown University, Father Orsy sees the Council as "a turning point" in the history of the church—one that will take "a long time to assimilate" and to fully appreciate in such areas as liturgy and the role of the laity. But he remains patient, and hopeful, that the "complex, complicated, beautiful vision of Vatican II" will be fully embraced in time.

GROWTH OF SOCIAL JUSTICE

In 1983 the bishops of the United States issued *The Challenge of Peace,* a pastoral letter on war and peace. In it they discussed the morality of war and of nuclear weapons. To help Catholics form their consciences on economic matters, they issued a pastoral letter on the U.S. economy in 1986. More recently, in 1999 and again in 2003, the U.S. bishops addressed civic responsibility in the document *Faithful Citizenship.*

Conscientious Catholics are reading these and other statements that the bishops have published on political and social issues. Church leaders continue to encourage Catholics to let their hearts be guided by the "social gospel."

Some people, however, are uncomfortable with the church's involvement in public issues. They criticize the church for "meddling in politics." Taking to heart the holistic view of salvation (discussed earlier) will help us see the mission of the church as healing unjust political structures and laws as well as unjust hearts.

Martin Luther King, Jr., illustrated this point during a speech in 1964 when he said: "The law cannot make a man love me, but it can keep him from lynching me!" King helps us see that Christians must seek to transform not only sinful hearts but also the sinful laws and customs of society that oppress and dehumanize our sisters and brothers.

Catholic social teaching reminds us that it is not enough to passively await God's kingdom in the next life. We are also called to make that kingdom present now, by working as God's instruments to remove injustice, discrimination, poverty and disease from our midst.

A TIME OF NEW GROWTH

What is happening in our church in these opening years of the third millennium? We are something like passengers in an airplane circling above the airport, waiting for the weather to clear so we can see to land.

What happened to the fast rate of change we experienced in those early years after the Council? The pace has certainly slowed. Church leaders seem to have decided that we need to take a break after so much turbulent change. We find ourselves in a time of consolidation and integration, taking stock of where we are.

One might compare the church to someone experiencing an identity crisis or confusing personal change. Such individuals need time to reflect and "get their act together" before moving on. Maybe the church leaders sense that it is time for the church to catch up with itself—to step back a bit and put all the pieces of our fragmented vision into a new whole. This need was satisfied to some degree with the issuing of the *Catechism of the Catholic Church,* but our Vatican II pilgrimage must always move forward.

No matter how carefully we try to put all the truths of the church into an orderly arrangement, we know that we must remain open to new questions needing new answers and to new challenges of growth from the Holy Spirit. Surely new roads lie before us!

A NEW LANGUAGE

signs of the times: a motto of Vatican II rooted in the church as sacrament, a visible sign of Jesus in the world. Pope John XXIII believed the church must change as the world changes. Related is *aggiornamento,* Italian for "updating." It refers to the spiritual renewal and institutional reform the Council sought to bring about.

ecumenical council: a meeting of the pope and the world's bishops (*ecumenical* is from the Greek for "universal") to make decisions for the church in matters of faith, morals, worship and discipline. The pope always presides over ecumenical councils and must confirm and promulgate decisions for them to be binding.

Questions for Discussion and Reflection

• What change in the church since the Second Vatican Council gives you the most encouragement about the church's future? If you lived through the changes, what was most difficult for you?

• How closely does the Vatican II vision of church match yours? In what ways does the church need to grow in order to continue embracing and working toward the vision set forth by the Council Fathers?

• What can you do to help keep the vision of Vatican II alive in your local church community?

CHAPTER TWO

The Mass: Our Greatest and Best Prayer

THOMAS RICHSTATTER, O.F.M.

What will the Catholic church of the next generation look like? The future shape of the Catholic church will be determined in large part by the decisions made at the Second Vatican Council. None of those decisions had a more immediate effect on Catholics than those regarding the Mass. The great majority of Catholics first experienced the fruits of Vatican II in their parish churches on Sunday mornings at the celebration of the Eucharist.

> The priest formerly said Mass *for* the people, now he celebrates the Eucharist *with* the people. And the faithful, for their part, are asked to move from *watching* to *doing*.

The essence of the Mass is, of course, timeless and changeless. But those of us old enough to remember the Sunday morning experience of the 1960s (no Saturday evening Masses then!) can testify that the Council radically changed the way we experience the Mass.

THE "GOOD OLD DAYS"

What was Mass like before the Council? If I close my eyes and remember the Latin Mass of my youth, the image that comes to mind is of a very reverent, mysterious, majestic ceremony unlike anything else in my daily life: different language, different garments, different gestures, different music (music that I can listen to now on CD performed by monks in great gothic churches). Everything pointed heavenward to the transcendent God of majesty.

I know enough about human nature to realize that this memory of sight and sound is perhaps more nostalgic than accurate. When remembering past events we often overlook the negative elements of the experience. This is especially true when imagining a past that one has not experienced personally.

THEN AND NOW

COUNCIL OF CHALCEDON (A.D. 451)

One of the burning issues of the early church—the relationship between Jesus' divinity and his humanity—was officially settled, if not immediately resolved, at the Council of Chalcedon. Meeting in the ancient city of Chalcedon in northwest Turkey, the bishops agreed to the definition that had been outlined by Pope Leo I. Jesus is one divine person, with a divine nature and a human nature. The two natures are distinct. Jesus is true God and true man, the Son of God and the son of Mary.

It took twenty-four days for the Council Fathers, most of them from the East, to come to agreement. But it would take far longer before heresies about the nature and being of Jesus would disappear. Chief among such heresies was Monophysitism, which held that there was but a single nature in Christ or that the human and divine in Christ constitute one composite nature. Another heresy held that Jesus' divine nature overwhelmed his human nature.

In 449 Pope Leo had tried to address the Monophysites at a synod in Ephesus, but his representatives were shouted down and unable to present the statement of faith he had prepared. Although he was not present at Chalcedon two years later, Leo's voice was finally heard. The minutes from the Council include the acclamation, "Peter has spoken through Leo."

For example, when I watch a cowboy movie I envy those men and their idyllic life on the prairie. They did not have to worry about publication deadlines, the stock market or college tuition. But where did they do their laundry? How did they get their teeth fixed? How did they recharge their cell phones?

A similar situation can arise when people "remember" the pre-Vatican II Mass, the Latin Masses read from a missal which, for the most part, was issued in 1570 after the Council of Trent. I have fond memories of those Latin Masses; they helped form my faith and nurture my vocation to the Franciscan Order and to the priesthood. But when I examine those memories critically, I find that the "good old days" were not totally good.

VERTICAL OR HORIZONTAL?

During high school and college I went to Mass to pray, but my prayer was not coordinated with the prayer of the priest at the altar. I was saying the rosary and other devotional prayers; the priest was saying the Mass. Of course, I stopped what I was doing and looked up at the ringing of the bell when the priest elevated the consecrated host. But other than that, the priest and I were not on the same page.

He was engaged in the official prayer of the church, the liturgy, which was primarily the worship of the transcendent God of majesty (a "vertical" action). I was saying the rosary and other devotional prayers—prayers that were more focused on my concerns (a "horizontal" action). The priest prayed in Latin, God's language; I prayed in English, my language.

The bishops of the Second Vatican Council tried to bring these "vertical" and "horizontal" prayers together into one. They realized that the worship that is most pleasing to God is the worship that brings us to our full spiritual, mental and physical potential. God cannot be worshiped (vertical) by those who are not concerned for others (horizontal).

Was the shift to a more "horizontal" liturgical style beneficial for our prayer and for our church? Some Catholics think that the worship of the transcendent God of majesty (the vertical) has become too folksy, too casual, too irreverent—too horizontal. Others feel that the "new" Mass is indeed reverent and mysterious but in a way that is different from the former ritual which, while very reverent, was also largely irrelevant to people's daily lives. They would say that the "old" Mass honored the Glorified Body of Christ in heaven without sufficient concern for Christ's Body on earth, the church.

This tension between the vertical and the horizontal is not new. Saint Paul tells the Corinthians that their eucharistic assemblies are "not for the better but for the worse" (1 Corinthians 11:17) because, while the community was attentive to the worship of God (the vertical), they did not connect that worship with care for the community, especially the poor (the horizontal).

A COMMON WORK

The Second Vatican Council's *Constitution on the Sacred Liturgy* states that the Mass is the work of the priest and people together. The faithful are to "take part fully aware of what they are doing, actively engaged in the rite and enriched by it" (11). The priest now speaks my language; I can understand the prayers. I can make the liturgical prayer my own and respond with faith: "Amen," "So be it," "Yes," "That's my prayer." I can see the face of the priest and he can see mine. I can follow his expressions of invitation, petition, praise and thanksgiving. I offer "the immaculate victim, not only through the hands of the priest but also together with him" (48).

Whereas the priest formerly said Mass *for* the people, now he celebrates the Eucharist *with* the people. *For* or *with*—small words, but a big change. And the faithful, for their part, are asked to move from *watching* to *doing*—again, a big change. And just as it takes more knowledge, skill and effort to *play* basketball than it does to *watch* a basketball game, it takes more knowledge, skill and effort to celebrate and participate in the Eucharist than it does to watch the priest say Mass. The "new" Mass brought with it new responsibilities.

ADDING HOLY THURSDAY TO GOOD FRIDAY

When I went to the Latin Masses years ago, I would imagine myself kneeling at the foot of the cross as Jesus died for my sins. I tried to offer my life as he offered his. I had learned from the *Baltimore*

Catechism: "The Mass is the sacrifice of the New Law in which Christ, through the ministry of the priest, offers Himself to God...." In the 1950s at most Masses no one other than the priest received Holy Communion. Even though Pope Pius X had encouraged frequent Communion in 1905, it took about fifty years for the practice to become common in American parishes. In the days when few people received Holy Communion, it was logical to describe the Mass in reference to Good Friday—sacrifice.

Vatican II wished to restore Holy Thursday to the picture: *"At the Last Supper, on the night he was betrayed,* our Savior instituted the eucharistic sacrifice of his body and blood" (*Constitution on the Sacred Liturgy* 47; emphasis added). Holy Thursday implies a meal—eating and drinking. But Catholics had been used to going to Mass for so many years without receiving Communion that, for many of us, Communion seemed something added to the sacrifice of the Mass. If it took decades for frequent Communion to become common practice, we can expect it to take a similar length of time for the "meal" dimension of the Eucharist to be integrated with the "sacrifice" dimension. Even today, many Catholics think of receiving Holy Communion in terms of their individual reception of the host rather than a communal sharing of a sacred meal.

At meals we eat *and drink.* Many Catholics have been so thoroughly taught that Christ is received whole and entire under the form of bread that they see no reason to drink from the cup. The *General Instruction of the Roman Missal* states: "Holy Communion has a fuller form as a sign when it is distributed under both kinds. For in this form the sign of the eucharistic banquet is more clearly evident and clear expression is given to the divine will by which the new and eternal Covenant is ratified in the Blood of the Lord, as also the relationship between the eucharistic banquet and the eschatological banquet in the Father's Kingdom" (281). We receive the bread, and we become the Body of Christ. The cup is the sign of how this comes about: Drinking the Blood of Christ, we pledge our willingness to pour out *our blood, our lives,* in service to one another—even as Christ did on the cross.

GETTING PERSONAL
JOSEPH KOMONCHAK

When he went to Rome in 1960 to begin the last phase of his studies for the priesthood, Joseph Komonchak couldn't have known that he was about to live through one of the most important and exciting times in church history. As a student at the Gregorian University, he was in a prime spot to catch the latest news as preparations for the Second Vatican Council were getting under way (1960–1962) and during its first two fall sessions (1962 and 1963).

Then only a "lowly seminarian," as he recently recalled, he (and his fellow students) had to be content with the understated Vatican press releases as the primary source of information about Council proceedings. Shy on specifics at first, the releases improved as Vatican II progressed. So did Joseph Komonchak's ability to read between the lines and piece together the various points of view vying for attention among the Council Fathers. "Our hopes would go up and down. It was a real roller coaster," he said. "It was a revolution in many ways."

Following his 1963 ordination in Rome for the Archdiocese of New York, Father Komonchak returned to the U.S. He was soon assigned to a parish that began implementing the documents of Vatican II. For the past twenty-seven years he has served as professor of theology at the Catholic University of America. One of his undergraduate courses, Vatican II: History and Theology, "fills up rapidly every time," said the sixty-five-year-old priest. "The Second Vatican Council has a mythic quality for my students; they are eager to learn what it was really about."

THE SIGN OF THE EUCHARISTIC BANQUET

For the reforms of the Second Vatican Council to bear fruit, the "sign of the eucharistic banquet" must be evident at every Mass. What does a banquet look like? This is a difficult question for those accustomed to fast food, eating alone or snacking in front of the TV. We can forget that a meal is more than just consuming food. Think of Thanksgiving dinner. While your family likely has its own particular customs, I expect that the general shape of the celebration is fourfold:

1. The extended family gathers together.
2. We catch up on news and family happenings.
3. We move to the table, say grace, and eat and drink.
4. We say our good-byes and return to our family homes.

The eucharistic banquet has this same fourfold shape, and this meal "shape" of the Eucharist has changed what we do at Mass:

1. First of all, we gather. We come together with other members of the parish.
2. We listen to the Scriptures and the homily. We hear of God's wondrous deeds and are moved to gratitude.
3. We place ourselves at the Lord's table with the apostles and all those who have shared the Eucharist throughout the centuries. We join with the priest in remembering the great deeds of salvation and ask the Father to send the Holy Spirit to change the bread and wine—and to change *us*—into Christ's Body: "Grant that we, who are nourished by his body and blood, may be filled with his Holy Spirit, and become one body, one spirit in Christ" (Eucharistic Prayer III). And then we come forward to eat the bread and drink from the cup.
4. Finally we are sent forth to live the mystery we have celebrated: to be Christ's body for the world, to feed the hungry,

give drink to the thirsty, welcome the stranger, clothe the naked, care for the ill and visit the imprisoned (Matthew 25:35–36).

A NEW LANGUAGE

liturgy: the official public worship of the church. Our most central liturgy is the Mass or *Eucharist.* *Eucharist* is from the Greek for "thanksgiving." This term is used to refer both to the Mass and to Christ's body in the form of bread and wine.

vernacular: the common spoken language of a people. In church life the word refers to the language used in our public worship. Vatican II's *Constitution on the Sacred Liturgy* permitted a change from Latin to the vernacular in the Mass, sacraments and Liturgy of the Hours.

MORE THAN REARRANGING THE FURNITURE

The changes in the Mass brought about by the Second Vatican Council were not merely cosmetic. The arguments about things that might seem to be superficial—the various opinions for or against Latin, inclusive language, kneeling, ministry, bowing at Communion—are actually about something much deeper, more important and much more elusive. They are about reverence, community and tradition. They touch deep-seated convictions about who we are as church, how God is to be worshiped and how we are to act in the world. It is the answers to these questions that will shape the church of future generations.

Questions for Discussion and Reflection

• What change in the Mass since the Second Vatican Council makes the most sense to you? If you lived through the changes, what was most difficult for you to understand? To adjust to?

• Is your current experience of liturgy more "vertical" or "horizontal"? How much do you think this depends on the priest and other parish leaders? On the members of the parish community?

• What will you do to increase your own full and active participation in the liturgy? How will you help encourage your community to participate more fully?

CHAPTER THREE
Seven Sacraments, One Mystery
THOMAS RICHSTATTER, O.F.M.

There were seven sacraments before the Second Vatican Council and there are seven sacraments after the Council. So what's different? Lots! We have moved from a system of seven rather unrelated "things" or objects to communal celebrations of personal encounter.

> Our understanding of sacrament starts with Jesus, then includes the church, the Eucharist, the other sacraments and sacramentals, until all creation is caught up in the wonderful revelation of the Creator.

THE CHURCH AS SACRAMENT
Vatican II reminded us of the biblical roots of the word "sacrament," namely, the wonderful, mysterious plan of God to save us through Christ Jesus. Sacraments are the visible, tangible manifestations of God's plan of salvation. They reveal what God is about and who God is. The fullness of this revelation is found in Jesus of Nazareth. We speak of Jesus as the "original" or "primal" sacrament; in him the invisible God became visible.

As a stone dropped into a pond causes ripples to go out in ever larger circles, our understanding of sacrament starts with Jesus, then includes the church, the Eucharist, the other sacraments and sacramentals, until all creation is caught up in the wonderful revelation of the Creator. Jesus passed through death to resurrection and breathed the Pentecost Spirit into the disciples. The church that grew out of the faith of the first Christians is the ongoing presence of Christ in our world. The church, the "Body of Christ," is called to be a sacrament, a sign and instrument of salvation.

The Council reminded us that the seven sacraments not only give grace but also build up the Body of Christ and are acts of worship. Because sacraments pertain to the whole church, the

Council stressed, "whenever rites...make provision for communal celebration involving the presence and active participation of the faithful, this way of celebrating them is to be preferred" (*Constitution on the Sacred Liturgy, Sacrosanctum Concilium,* 27).

Sacraments that were once celebrated privately are now often celebrated publicly at Sunday Eucharist or in other communal settings. For example, when an infant is baptized, the baptism is not just for the baby; it is a communal act of worship and an occasion of grace for the whole community.

THEN AND NOW
COUNCIL OF CONSTANCE (1414–1418)

Controversy swirled from beginning to end at the Council of Constance, which met in southern Germany during a troubled period in church history. When the Council opened, three men claimed to be pope. A short time later the one who had called the Council fled—in disguise—when he realized he would not retain power. By the time the Council concluded, the Great Western Schism that had long divided the church had been resolved and a new pope, Martin V, had been unanimously elected to lead the church as the sole pontiff.

Church historians have raised questions about the authority of the Council of Constance, which was convened by a so-called antipope amid chaos and intrigue. As a result, some of its enactments have been called into question. This includes a decree that held that the Council had supremacy over the pope—a clear threat to papal authority. This idea was later rejected. In addition, the churchmen, theologians and princes who attended the Council fumbled through other agenda items, including church reform and heretical teachings.

Martin V, the "Restorer of Rome," is the Council's crowning achievement.

EUCHARIST

The Second Vatican Council speaks of the Eucharist before discussing any of the other sacraments. The Eucharist is the *first sacrament*, the source and summit of Christian life. When it comes to revealing who God is, the Eucharist says it all. We are never more church than when we are celebrating the Eucharist.

Each of the other sacraments is an aspect of the central, eucharistic mystery—a celebration of the revelation that God created us because God loves us. The Eucharist is the model for all the sacraments. The shape of the Eucharist (gathering, storytelling, meal sharing and commissioning) is the model shape for all the other sacraments.

BAPTISM AND CONFIRMATION

Before Vatican II we seldom spoke of baptism, confirmation and Eucharist in the same sentence, and we rarely celebrated them in the same ritual as we do now at the Easter Vigil. Together these three sacraments *initiate* us into a community of faith, a eucharistic community. We call them the Sacraments of Initiation.

Before the Council, a shortened form of the *Rite of Baptism of Adults* was used for infant baptism. The Council called for a new rite for the baptism of children; this rite acknowledges the parents' role in presenting their child for baptism and their responsibility for raising their child in the faith. Changes in this rite also flow from the *Constitution on the Sacred Liturgy*, which says that communal forms of sacraments are preferred (27). This is why children are often baptized during Sunday Eucharist.

Another new rite is the *Rite of Christian Initiation of Adults*, commonly called the RCIA. When adults are baptized, they celebrate baptism and confirmation and then are invited to share in the Eucharist. Celebrating the Sacraments of Initiation in their original order—baptism, confirmation, Eucharist—more clearly expresses that it is Eucharist that completes our Christian initiation (*Catechism of the Catholic Church*, #1322). An increasing number of dioceses are restoring this original sequence of the initiation sacraments for those baptized as infants.

The bishops at the Second Vatican Council directed that the *Rite of Confirmation* also be revised so that "the intimate connection which this sacrament has with the whole of Christian initiation...be more clearly set forth" (*Constitution on the Sacred Liturgy*, 71). Whenever it is celebrated, the meaning of confirmation is best explained and understood in its relationship to the other Sacraments of Initiation—baptism and Eucharist.

RECONCILIATION

The sacrament of reconciliation (also known as confession or penance) has undergone more changes over time than any other sacrament. In the first centuries of the church, most Catholics never celebrated the sacrament. In the 1940s and 1950s we saw long lines of Catholics waiting to go to Saturday confession. The Council documents include only one sentence about the revision of this sacrament, calling for the rite and formulas to "more clearly express both the nature and effect of the sacrament" (*Constitution on the Sacred Liturgy*, 72). The general principles of the Council (such as, Eucharist as the model for all sacraments, Scripture having an important role in all sacraments, sacraments being public in nature and so on) were applied in revising this sacrament.

While the opportunity for individual celebrations is still available today, communal celebrations have become common and are often celebrated in packed churches. We have also moved to calling the sacrament "reconciliation" rather than confession or penance as we did in the past. This word change reflects a change in focus—from what *we* do (confess our sins, do a penance) to what *God* does (reconcile us).

ANOINTING OF THE SICK

Before the Council, the sacrament of anointing was known as Extreme Unction, the anointing *(unction)* for persons at the point of death *(in extremis)*. We now speak of the sacrament of the anointing of the sick, indicating that this sacrament is intended for *all* who are seriously ill. As we embrace a more holistic view of health and wellness, we pray not only for physical healing but also for mental and spiritual healing.

As sacraments are acts of public worship, anointing is no longer primarily celebrated privately. Communal celebrations of this sacrament during Eucharist are widespread. The celebration of this sacrament speaks of our dying with Christ—the dying we vowed in baptism. It is a sign of our acceptance of the cross of Christ, that health and productivity are not the main criteria for judging human worth. These signs are important for the entire community to witness and celebrate.

MARRIAGE

The Council brought about two major changes in our understanding of the sacrament of marriage. First, the Council speaks of marriage as a "covenant." The marriage *covenant* helps us think in biblical and interpersonal categories that reach beyond the legal categories of the marriage *contract*. The marriage covenant is a symbol of God's covenant with humanity.

Second, the Council taught that the purpose of marriage is not only to produce children but also to enable the couple to support one another in mutual love. Marriage is an "intimate partnership" of life and love (*Church in the Modern World*, 48). We look to the married couple as a sacrament, a sign to the world of God's love.

Both of these changes enrich our understanding of the sacrament of marriage. But they also open the door to new questions: Who is capable of a sacramental marriage? What are the qualities and conditions necessary for a marriage to be a sign of God's love for the church? In a time when Catholic marriages are vulnerable to the stresses of modern life, the church's support of married couples is vital.

GETTING PERSONAL
CARDINAL WILLIAM KEELER

When he was unexpectedly tapped in 1962 to go to Vatican II as priest-secretary to his bishop, Father William Keeler was urged, "Make yourself as useful as you can."

Over the next four years the young priest did just that, summarizing in English talks that had been delivered in Latin at Council sessions. The talks, published in the Council Digest, became an invaluable resource for English-speaking bishops and reporters. Along with others he also served on a press panel for journalists, offering daily briefings.

Now he is Cardinal Keeler, head of the Archdiocese of Baltimore, and his memories of Vatican II are still fresh. "It was enormously exciting to see things unfold" at the Council sessions, he said. "I saw a coming together of viewpoints— two thousand of them! People listened to each other in a spirit of faith. The Holy Spirit was at work."

More than once, then-Father Keeler saw proposed documents go through several drafts and major revisions. This included *The Dogmatic Constitution on the Church (Lumen Gentium)*, which was "legalistic" at the outset but, in final form, "was imbued with the language of Scripture and the early teachers of the church."

Asked about the unfinished business of Vatican II, Cardinal Keeler prefers to speak of "ongoing challenges." These include progress in ecumenical and interreligious relations. "There has to be peace among faith families before there can be peace among nations. That's the big challenge we haven't yet fully grasped: how important

it is that we are in dialogue with other Christians
and with other religions."

HOLY ORDERS

When we think of holy orders, we usually think of the sacrament
by which one becomes a priest. But holy orders ends in "s" because
it names *three* sacramental orders: the Order of the Episcopate
(bishops), the Order of Presbyters (priests) and the Order of
Deacons. The Council had important things to say about each of
these.

The Order of the Episcopate (Bishops). The Council affirmed that a
bishop is ordained to the fullness of the sacrament of orders. By
his ordination a bishop becomes a member of the College of
Bishops and assumes responsibility not only for his own local
church but also for the universal church.

The Order of Presbyters (Priests). We have all witnessed the drastic
decline in the number of priests. Empty rectories, merged
parishes, closed seminaries, "Sunday Celebrations in the Absence
of a Priest"—the bishops of Vatican II envisioned none of these
things.

The Council made two major changes that radically affected
the lives of priests. First, while the ordained have specific ministries within the church, the Council affirmed that the basis of all
ministry is baptism into the Body of Christ. Second, the Council
placed the priest *in the midst* of the baptized and said that priests
should "work together with the lay faithful" (*Decree on the Ministry
and Life of Priests, Presbyterorum Ordinis,* 9).

To go from being "set apart from the faithful" to living "in the
midst of the faithful" was a big change. The Council affirmed that
priests are in a certain sense "set apart" but they are not to be "separated" from the People of God because priests cannot serve the
faithful if they are strangers to their lives and conditions (*Decree on
the Ministry and Life of Priests,* 3). Has this change in identity contributed to the decline in the number of priests?

The Order of Deacons. Deacons had ministered in the Western church until about the fifth century. By the time of the Second Vatican Council, the Order of Deacons was simply a transitional stage for those "passing through" on their way to the priesthood. The Council restored the Order of Deacons, making it a permanent ministry in the church. The bishops of the Council decided to permit married men to be ordained deacons. In 1967 there were no permanent deacons; today there are over thirty thousand deacons worldwide.

A NEW LANGUAGE

catechumenate: a period in the church's process of preparing adults for entrance into the church. This term is often used interchangeably with the name of the entire process, the *Rite of Christian Initiation of Adults* (RCIA). Both date back to the first centuries of the church and were restored after Vatican II.

communal penance: a group celebration of the sacrament of penance (confession/reconciliation). The most common form includes a communal prayer service with individual confession and absolution. Communal celebrations help us see that sin is not private but affects the community.

CONCLUSION

We seem to have more questions about the sacraments today than we had before the Council: What is the proper age for confirmation? Will the individual rite of confession disappear altogether? What will happen to marriage and family life if annulments continue to increase in number? How can we remain a eucharistic church with fewer priests?

Did the Council cause more problems than it solved? It did not intend to solve problems but to adapt the liturgy and the sacraments to the needs of our times (*Constitution on the Sacred Liturgy*, 1). The needs of the times have changed in the years since the Council and will continue to change. There will always be unfinished business.

But rather than wringing our hands, we need to demonstrate the same hope and courage that the Holy Spirit inspired at the Council. The bishops stated, "...the church constantly moves forward toward the fullness of divine truth" (*Constitution on Divine Revelation*, 8). We have not yet arrived; we are still on the journey. The road may be difficult at times, but with the faith of Saint Paul we are confident "that the one who began a good work among you will bring it to completion by the day of Jesus Christ" (Philippians 1:6).

Questions for Discussion and Reflection

• What does it mean to say that the church is a sacrament? How does this affect your understanding of the seven sacraments?

• How well has your parish embraced the shift from private to communal celebrations of sacraments (for example, baptism during Sunday Mass, communal penance services, community celebrations of anointing of the sick)? What has your community gained from these changes?

• How can you grow in understanding of the sacraments, especially those that have changed in your lifetime?

CHAPTER FOUR

Sacred Scripture: Light for Our Path

DIANNE BERGANT, C.S.A.

In the years leading up to the Second Vatican Council, the Bible played a relatively small role in the lives of most Catholics. Few Catholics were directly acquainted with its content except for the Bible stories they learned in their catechism classes and the readings they heard the priest proclaim on Sundays or major feast days. Even then, a sermon based on these readings was rare. Sermons were usually about church teaching or practice.

> As important as it is to know what the Bible originally meant, we must also be concerned about what it might mean in today's world—a world embroiled in economic injustice, war and discrimination.

Before Vatican II many people even felt that it was dangerous to read the Bible without the explicit direction of the church. Protestants may have been versed in biblical knowledge, but not Catholics. In fact, many Catholics considered reading the Bible a Protestant devotion.

Circumstances are quite different today. Even those Catholics whose only experience of religious practice is Sunday or feast day Masses have come to know quite a bit about the Bible. The liturgy is full of biblical themes, we sing songs based on Bible passages, and most homilies relate to the readings of the day. Many people today look to Sacred Scripture for inspiration and guidance in their life decisions.

TURNING TO THE BIBLE

The Second Vatican Council spearheaded a marvelous revitalizing of the Bible in the church. Both during and between its four general sessions, many Council Fathers attended lectures given by prominent biblical scholars. This prepared them to consider biblical revelation as they made decisions at the Council. Another indication of the Council's "turn to the Bible" is that the Book of the Gospels was given a central place in the room where the Council Fathers often gathered for general sessions.

In 1965 the *Dogmatic Constitution on Divine Revelation (Dei Verbum)* helped us see the importance of using the tools of history and literature to achieve a better understanding of the Bible. The language in which the text was written, the culture and times of the author, and the religious concerns of the people for whom it was originally written were now to be taken into account. (The biblical study methods that consider these elements are called "critical" approaches—not in the negative sense of "criticizing" but that of "looking carefully.")

Interest now focused on the meaning intended by the original author, not just on the literal meaning of the words. It was almost as if the Bible had been reborn and those involved in any form of Bible study were reborn with it. The study of the Bible became exciting and uncovered a profound hunger for the Word of God among the People of God.

This hunger was evident in a phenomenon known as the "base Christian community." All over the world small groups of ordinary Christians were meeting to discuss how the message of the Bible could make a difference in their lives and call them to action. Although they often had a group leader, the members were seldom trained in any form of biblical interpretation. However, this did not deter them. They studied and they prayed. Various degrees of social awareness grew out of these groups. Today similar groups can be found in parishes around the world.

THEN AND NOW
COUNCIL OF NICAEA (A.D. 787)

For more than a century, bitter debate raged in the church about the meaning and proper use of sacred images. The controversy was especially intense in the East, where religious images such as statues, crosses and icons were destroyed by order of the Byzantine emperors. Those who followed this thinking were called *iconoclasts* (Greek for "smashers of images"). They aimed to halt what they saw as idolatry, pointing to the Old Testament prohibition against making "idols." They also saw veneration of such images as an impediment to the conversion of Jews and Muslims and believed that images depicting Jesus' human form represented an assault of sorts on his divinity.

The Empress Irene of Constantinople called the Second Council of Nicaea to return the church in the East to the tradition of venerating sacred images, including icons. Pope Adrian I sent a delegation of two from Rome, while 350 Byzantine bishops participated. Nicaea II validated the practice of venerating images of Jesus, Mary and the saints but distinguished between the adoration due to God alone and the honoring of sacred images. Reception of the Council's rulings was slow in the East, even more so in the West.

FEEDING THE HUNGER

This grassroots movement was beginning at the same time that the documents of Vatican II were being released to the faithful. People gradually came to realize the importance of more serious biblical study. Graduate programs sprang up across the United States and beyond. These programs were usually open to laypeople. Seminaries began to revise their courses of study. No longer was the Bible taught primarily as a way of reinforcing specific doctrines. It was now studied from an entirely different point of view: to seek our best understanding of God's revelation through the Word.

The Council recommended that "easy access to Sacred Scripture...be provided to the Christian faithful" (*Dogmatic Constitution on Divine Revelation*, 22) and that a "warm and living love for Scripture" be promoted (*Constitution on the Sacred Liturgy*, 24). As a result, catechetical programs grounded in the Bible were established in parishes, a three-year lectionary cycle introduced the people to more readings, homilies were rooted in Sacred Scripture and several translations of the Bible appeared with study helps. The Bible itself ceased to be only a family heirloom showcased on the coffee table and became a well-worn, dog-eared, frequently consulted best-seller.

The development of a more analytical and critical approach to Catholic biblical scholarship actually began long before Vatican II. In 1893 Pope Leo XIII acknowledged some of the achievements of Protestant scholars in this area. He later established the Pontifical Biblical Commission. This group of biblical scholars has recently addressed such topics as the distinctions between historical fact and truth in Scripture; how we as a church should interpret Scripture; and how ancient writings, sacred to the Jews, should also be regarded as Christian texts. In 1943 Pope Pius XII wrote the first document devoted entirely to the church's position on biblical interpretation and opened a new era in Catholic scholarship.

UNITING ALL GOD'S PEOPLE

In the past, the Bible often divided Catholics and Protestants. When differences in understanding Scripture occur now, they are more likely the result of the method used in reading the Bible than of the church to which one belongs. Some people choose analytical or critical methods to discover the meaning of biblical texts; others base their interpretation of passages on the literal meaning of the words only.

Since Vatican II the study of the Bible enjoys considerable cooperation among Christian churches. This ecumenical and interfaith cooperation is evident in the membership of biblical translation committees. Christians, and sometimes Jews, are found on these committees. There are also written commentaries that are popular among both scholars and ordinary churchgoers.

In its most recent document, *The Interpretation of the Bible in the Church* (1994), the Pontifical Biblical Commission insisted that, as important as it is to know what the Bible originally meant, we must also be concerned about what it might mean in today's world—a world embroiled in economic injustice, war and discrimination. This means that, in our reading of the Bible, we must be sensitive to issues of gender, race, ethnic origin, class and other political factors that make up the real world. These factors influence the way women and men perceive reality and fashion their inner and outer worlds.

Such sensitivity is particularly difficult to develop when we read stories that are clearly biased in favor of one group over another. For example, the Israelites are too often chosen over the Egyptians, men preferred to women, and physical disabilities considered a form of punishment for sin. One of the pressing issues facing us today is the challenge to be faithful to the meaning of the biblical narrative while at the same time considering how we understand things in the world today.

We have come a long way in the area of sensitivity. The liberation theology movement that appeared in Latin America in the early 1970s has significantly affected the way we read the Bible. The experience of oppression and poverty brought people to a new appreciation of the Bible stories of liberation. This in turn has inspired many people to challenge governmental structures and policies that they believe to be unjust. Related to this are the women's movement and its concern for inclusive language in both biblical translations and the prayers used during liturgies. Some dismiss inclusive language as being merely a matter of political correctness. But is it not rather about recognizing the equality of all before God?

GETTING PERSONAL
SISTER MARY LUKE TOBIN, S.L.

Picture it: It's autumn 1964. A religious sister in full habit is standing on the deck of an ocean liner heading to Europe. She is on her way to the Second Vatican Council, determined that women's voices will be heard.

Meet Sister of Loretto Mary Luke Tobin, one of only fifteen women auditors from around the world invited to Vatican II. President of her religious community and of the Conference of Major Superiors of Women during the Council, she attended its third and fourth sessions in Rome.

"It was important that women be observers, if not participants," says Sister Mary Luke, who turned ninety-six last month. "Women are half the church," she said. "We had to be there...as part of the living, speaking church."

She was honored by being named to Vatican II commissions that planned the documents on the church in the modern world and on the laity. "I was not pushy, but I was no shrinking violet either. It was a learning experience for the bishops, but they got used to me," she said impishly.

The Denver native credits Vatican II with "bringing the church into the world" and taking the first steps toward a true appreciation of women's gifts and contributions to the church. "It was a privilege for me to be at Vatican II and for women to have part in it.

"The Council was an important step forward, but we still have some distance to go," she says.

And what comes then? "Vatican III will look back and build on Vatican II."

LOOKING TO THE FUTURE

What can we expect from biblical study in the future? Two topics come to mind: biblical translations and sensitivity to the integrity of creation.

As already mentioned, the question of inclusive language is a burning issue for some in the church today. A particularly challenging aspect of the translation question involves how we refer to

God. Sacred Scripture uses male adjectives and pronouns when referring to God. On the other hand, it does at times use descriptions of God that are feminine. We are expected to understand the words used as inclusive in spite of our language's limitations to fully express them as such. At present, the official church decision concerning biblical texts used in liturgy is to maintain the established gender usage. This means that we can expect to continue hearing mostly masculine references to God in our liturgies.

While the church can make decisions about the language used in our Bible translations and liturgies, personal images of God cannot be limited. Many people, women and men alike, find viewing and relating to God as both masculine and feminine to be important for their growth as persons of faith. There are many sides to this issue, and people fervently argue for each of them.

People may view this as a gender issue, but it carries broader significance. It is probably true that sensitivity to gender-specific language spearheaded this concern, but it has expanded to uncovering bias in other biblical expressions. For example, a passage from the Song of Songs has traditionally been translated: "I am black, but beautiful" (1:5). The conjunction "but" suggests an exception, implying that black is not normally beautiful. A bias becomes evident when we learn that the Hebrew conjunction used can also be translated "and." This yields a very different meaning. A need for sensitivity to racial issues is clear, and many contemporary translations of the Bible do use "and" rather than "but."

Another topic for future study is the biblical understanding of the relationship between humankind and the rest of the natural world. Current threats to ecological balance have forced a new look at the biblical foundation of our attitude toward the planet earth. The passage that is probably responsible for much of the misunderstanding of this matter is the order given by God at the time of creation: "...subdue it; and have dominion over..." (Genesis 1:28). This command has led some to believe that the natural world is under the sovereign control of human beings who can do with it what they wish. This interpretation leads to an attitude of disregard and exploitation. We need to place this passage from Genesis alongside others that sketch a different perspective such as: "The earth is the LORD's" (Psalm 24:1).

The current concern for ecology has called for a reexamination of the biblical stories of creation as well as other passages dealing with natural creation. We now see that many of our attitudes toward natural creation have been grounded in faulty reading of the biblical accounts. The development of an authentic biblical theology of ecology is now in its infancy, but many believe that this topic will open up an exciting field of examination and spirituality.

The Council threw the door to Scripture study wide open. Women and men, lay and ordained, have committed themselves to various forms of biblical study and ministry and have been enriched in ways far beyond their own imagining. What does the future hold? Stay tuned!

A NEW LANGUAGE

Liturgy of the Word: the part of the Mass during which God's word in Sacred Scripture is proclaimed. It consists of Bible readings, a psalm and the Gospel Acclamation. The homily, Profession of Faith and General Intercessions further develop and conclude the Liturgy of the Word.

lectionary: the book from which the Scripture readings for Sunday and weekday Masses are proclaimed. The lectionary is found in several volumes. They include a three-year cycle for Sunday and solemn feast readings, a two-year weekday cycle, a one-year cycle for saints' feasts, readings for other Masses, Responsorial Psalms and Gospel Acclamations.

Questions for Discussion and Reflection

• What has been your reaction to the changes that new biblical study methods have brought to the way we read and interpret Scripture? Have you welcomed these changes? How have you been challenged by them?

• How well is your parish community promoting growth in "a warm and living love for Scripture"?

• Have you taken advantage of local opportunities to grow in your knowledge and understanding of the Bible? What more might you do in the future?

CHAPTER FIVE
Catholicism Welcomes the World
Virginia Smith

Tucked away among the longer documents of Vatican II are two shorter ones: the *Decree on Ecumenism* and the *Declaration on the Relation of the Church to Non-Christian Religions.* Their impact far exceeds their length. Together with the *Declaration on Religious Freedom,* these landmark documents represent a great leap forward for the church, creating a seismic shift that will continue to reverberate across the religious world in the decades and centuries ahead.

> We discover who we are only by engaging those different from ourselves. This helps us to clarify and articulate our faith, making dialogue a spiritual discipline.

Unity, especially among Christians, was a theme of the papacy of John XXIII. He wanted to change the long-standing attitude of Catholic triumphalism that stood in the way of better relations with other denominations. When the pope declared his intention to convene the ecumenical council, it was clear that ecumenism would be a pivotal theme.

Many people mistakenly think John XXIII's commitment to ecumenism is the reason behind calling Vatican II "ecumenical." In fact, the word *ecumenical* simply refers to something universal or general in scope—thus its use to describe the Council. It has also come to mean cooperation and communication within the worldwide Christian community. Some mention of ecumenism from that perspective found its way into eight of the sixteen documents of Vatican II as well as the opening speeches of both Council popes, John XXIII and Paul VI.

Perhaps most remarkable was the invitation extended to other Christian churches to send representatives to the Council. Twenty-one Orthodox and Protestant groups accepted the invitation, including Russian Orthodox, Anglican, Lutheran, Friends

(Quakers), Congregational, Methodist, Presbyterian, Disciples of Christ and the World Council of Churches.

THEN AND NOW

LATERAN V (1512–1517)

Strong winds of discontent were blowing during the early part of the sixteenth century—both inside and outside the church.

Pope Julius II convened Lateran V in Rome to undercut bishops participating in another church council then in session at Pisa. (The pope's opponents, frustrated at his failure to call a council in a timely manner, had gone ahead and were meeting without him.) Initially, the Council Fathers at Lateran V kept a close eye on Pisa, condemning its decrees and dismissing it as counterfeit. Even after Pisa had ended and Pope Julius died, the Council spent more time worrying about restrictions on papal authority than confronting the really serious issues facing the church, beginning with a corrupt papacy. It did attempt some reforms—condemning the buying or selling of church offices and lending money at exorbitant interest rates; warning against false preachers, sorcery and blasphemy; trying to control errors against the faith in print. But it accomplished little.

The new pope, Leo X, and the Fathers at Lateran V missed the forest for the trees. Six months after the Council ended in March 1517, Martin Luther nailed his ninety-five theses on the door of the castle church at Wittenburg.

MOVING TOWARD CHRISTIAN UNITY

When the draft of the *Decree on Ecumenism* was introduced to the Council, the bishops' reaction was immediate and enthusiastic. Montreal's Cardinal Léger remarked, "The present hope for and movement toward unity are not passing impulses, but are inspired by the Gospel and the Holy Spirit."

Initially, questions concerning non-Christian religions and religious liberty were included in the *Decree on Ecumenism*. It was decided to treat these unique issues in separate documents. This allowed the *Decree on Ecumenism* to focus exclusively on the regrettable divisions in the Body of Christ.

In a move startling to some, the decree sought to re-establish ties with other Christian traditions rather than insist that they embrace Catholicism. Equally astonishing was the admission that the Catholic church shares the responsibility for existing divisions and sees its own reform as an essential component in efforts toward reunion. To this end, the decree made a strong push for dialogue and opened the door to friendly discourse by acknowledging separated Christian traditions as sister and brother churches.

BUILDING THE BODY OF CHRIST

Focusing first on what unites Christians rather than the sometimes serious issues dividing them, the church let it be known that many important elements that

> build up and give life to the church itself, can exist outside the visible boundaries of the Catholic church: the written Word of God; the life of grace; faith, hope, and charity, with the other interior gifts of the Holy Spirit.... Our separated brothers and sisters also carry out many liturgical actions of the Christian religion...these liturgical actions most certainly can truly engender a life of grace, and...are capable of giving access to that communion in which is salvation. (3)

Lest Catholicism be seen as setting itself above the fray, the Council Fathers acknowledged:

Catholics must assuredly be concerned for the members of separated Christian communities, praying for them, keeping them informed about the church, making the first approaches toward them. But their primary duty is to make a careful and honest appraisal of whatever needs to be renewed and done in the Catholic household itself, in order that its life may bear witness more clearly and more faithfully to the teachings and institutions which have been handed down from Christ through the apostles. (4)

Vatican II recognized that efforts toward unity were not entirely new. "Already this renewal is taking place in various spheres of the church's life: the biblical and liturgical movements; the preaching of the Word of God and catechetics; the apostolate of the laity; new forms of religious life and the spirituality of married life; and the church's social teaching and activity" (6).

In the final analysis, much of the work of ecumenism begins with individuals: "The faithful should remember that they promote union among Christians better, that indeed they live it better, when they try to live holier lives according to the Gospel" (7).

TURNING TOWARD EACH OTHER

Opinions about how far we've traveled toward Christian unity differ widely. As in most other major areas addressed by the Council Fathers, the opinion pendulum swings from those who believe too little has been accomplished to those who consider the church to have gone too far.

Those who would like to see more rapid progress may well mean more *obvious* progress. The years immediately following the Council saw teeming activity with everything from ecumenical discussion groups to joint prayer gatherings. In their eagerness to be accommodating, some people tended to ignore very real differences between Catholics and their fellow Christians. By now, most sincere people realize that nothing is gained by refusing to acknowledge points on which we disagree.

While it is probably true that the initial fervor has cooled a bit, that in no way implies that the work of ecumenism has stalled. In the years since the Council, Catholic theologians and scholars have met for weeks, months and even years with their counterparts from other traditions including Anglican, Orthodox, Lutheran and Methodist. Their work is true ecumenism, first seeking points of accord and harmony, then recognizing legitimate areas of difference and finally searching for common ground on critical positions.

During a recent discussion in Rome on ecumenical relations, Australian Bishop Michael Putney, who cochairs the International Methodist-Catholic Dialogue, commented that Vatican II had converted him to the cause of ecumenism. He added that we discover who we are only by engaging those different from ourselves. This helps us to clarify and articulate our faith, making dialogue a spiritual discipline.

Are we there yet? Certainly not. But after centuries of moving ever farther apart, Christians have at last turned toward one another. That may be the most important effect of the *Decree on Ecumenism* over time, for direction is more important than speed.

FINDING TRUTH IN OTHER FAITHS

In a single chapter, *The Declaration on the Relation of the Church to Non-Christian Religions* turned centuries of disregard and, too often, disrespect a full 180 degrees. The declaration (commonly referred to by its Latin title, *Nostra Aetate*) was originally intended to focus almost exclusively on Catholic-Jewish relations, a topic dear to the heart of Pope John XXIII. As apostolic delegate to Turkey and Greece during World War II, he had helped Jewish refugees fleeing to Palestine. He came away from that experience determined that anti-Semitism, wherever and however it still existed in the world, must be stamped out. In its final form the declaration still carried a heavy Jewish focus but was broadened to include other great traditions as well.

Here, for the first time, the Catholic church conceded that, while the fullness of truth rests in Jesus, much truth is to be found and respected in other religions also. Equally radical was the document's encouragement of dialogue among the great world faiths and recognition of the contributions they have made.

CHANGING ATTITUDES

For the first time in its history, the Catholic church formally expressed appreciation for the merits of non-Christian religions: "The Catholic church rejects nothing of what is true and holy in these religions. It has a high regard for the manner of life and conduct, the precepts and doctrines which...often reflect a ray of that truth which enlightens all..." (2).

In light of recent world events, the following has taken on more vital significance: "The church has also a high regard for the Muslims. They worship God, who is one, living and subsistent, merciful and almighty, the Creator of heaven and earth.... Although not acknowledging him as God, they venerate Jesus as a prophet; his virgin Mother they also honor, and even at times devoutly invoke" (3).

And after a long history of persecutions and pogroms carried out against Jews on the grounds that they are Christ-killers, the declaration reads:

Even though the Jewish authorities and those who followed their lead pressed for the death of Christ (see John 19:6), neither all Jews indiscriminately at that time, nor Jews today, can be charged with the crimes committed during his passion.... Remembering, then, its common heritage with the Jews and moved not by any political consideration, but solely by the religious motivation of Christian charity, it deplores all hatreds, persecutions, displays of anti-Semitism levelled at any time or from any source against the Jews. (4)

RESPECTING OTHERS

Pope John Paul II did much to forward the agenda of Vatican II's declaration on non-Christian religions: gathering the leaders of many faiths at Assisi, praying at Auschwitz and joining Jerusalem's rabbinical leaders in prayer at the Western (Wailing) Wall. He was also the first pope in history to enter and pray in a mosque.

In the days and weeks following 9/11, I received many phone calls and E-mails from former students, expressing gratitude that they had some knowledge of Islam. Many were surprised and dismayed to find they were the only ones in their circles of friends and coworkers who had some acquaintance with Muslim belief and practice. They acted as voices crying in the wilderness, trying to explain that what occurred that dreadful day in no way reflected authentic Islamic teaching.

Gradually, Catholics are grasping the truth that every religion, including their own, contains extreme groups that do not accurately reflect their tradition's beliefs.

What the *Decree on Ecumenism* and the *Declaration on the Relation of the Church to Non-Christian Religions* require of all religious persons of good will is twofold: to understand *accurately* and respect other religious traditions, and to reflect in our own lives an authentic image of our own tradition. In that way, we will honor both the innovative Council documents we have examined here and the pope whose astonishing vision we have to thank for them.

GETTING PERSONAL

RABBI LEON KLENICKI

Leon Klenicki was thousands of miles away from Rome when Vatican II was in session, but he felt its impact as if he were there in the thick of it.

Then a rabbinical student at Hebrew Union College in Cincinnati, he stayed informed about Council proceedings through reading and joining lively discussions on campus with fellow students and professors. "There were two camps about the Council at that time," Rabbi Klenicki recently said:

"Rome is never going to change" and "Hey, this is serious."

He himself was somewhere in between, "doubtful but hopeful." Looking back now, he sees Vatican II as "a real revolution. I was taken aback by the church opening itself to the world and to non-Catholics." *Nostra Aetate* was "the beginning of the reclaiming of the Roman Catholic soul with regard to Jews and Judaism."

A native of Buenos Aires, Rabbi Klenicki has kept a close watch ever since, particularly in his role as director of the department of interfaith affairs for the Anti-Defamation League. (He's now a consultant.) Through his writing and teaching, he's also helped keep alive the revolution in interfaith relations begun at Vatican II. He welcomes efforts that have followed it, including practical suggestions for implementing *Nostra Aetate*, guidelines about how to present Jews and Judaism in church preaching and increased focus on the Holocaust.

Still, Rabbi Klenicki hopes for more: for Catholics, "total implementation" of Vatican II teachings about Judaism; for Jews, "a more serious appreciation of the meaning of Christianity in God's design."

A NEW LANGUAGE

separated brothers and sisters: a way to refer to baptized Christians who are not Catholics; this phrase acknowledges that, although differences divide us, we are all part of one family in Christ.

salvation outside the church: the recognition that God's saving power is extended to all who sincerely seek God and those who may not know of God but who strive to live a good life (*Lumen Gentium*, 16). While still maintaining the Catholic church's centrality, we acknowledge that our savior "desires everyone to be saved and to come to the knowledge of the truth" (1 Timothy 2:4).

Questions for Discussion and Reflection

• What is your attitude toward people of other Christian traditions? People of other faiths? Is this based on personal experience, study or hearsay?

• The Council Fathers challenge us as a church and as individuals to make our lives bear faithful witness to the teachings of Christ. How well does your life reflect an authentic image of our Catholic tradition?

• Have you taken advantage of opportunities to grow in knowledge and accurate understanding of other religious traditions? What more might you do in the future?

CHAPTER SIX
Called to Holiness and Service: Ordained Ministry
BISHOP ROBERT F. MORNEAU

Through baptism all of God's people are called to holiness. Jesus said, "I am the vine, you are the branches...apart from me you can do nothing" (John 15:5). Holiness is this intimate connection with the Lord. It is a friendship with God leading to a fruitful and productive life. Priestly ministry will be effective in proportion to the holiness of the ordained.

> Never before has there been such a need for courageous, discerning hearts to keep the priest and his people grounded in gospel values.

The Second Vatican Council gave major consideration to the ordained ministry of deacons, priests and bishops in three of its sixteen documents. In them the Council Fathers looked intently at both the life and ministry of those ordained for service to God's people.

The focus of our reflections here will be on the ministry of priesthood. Three questions will be addressed: What is the function of the priest in today's church? What is the cultural context in which priesthood is being lived out? What does the future look like for the priesthood?

CHANGING MINISTRY OF PRIESTS
A priest has four tasks: to proclaim the Good News of God's love and mercy, to preside at and celebrate the sacraments, to serve the local church community as servant-leader, and to reach out to all in need—both within and beyond one's own community. Some priests will be called to specialized ministries (administrators, chaplains, teachers, etc.), but all are ordained to proclaim, celebrate, serve and reach out.

In a sense this has always been the mission of the priest—before, during and after the Second Vatican Council. Yet our growing understanding of church as the whole people of God has altered how the priest goes about his tasks.

THEN AND NOW
COUNCIL OF EPHESUS (A.D. 431)

Is Jesus one person, human and divine, or two separate people somehow merged into one person? And what of Mary: Is she the mother of the human person Jesus or the mother of God?

These questions were still unsettled at the outset of the Council of Ephesus, one of the more raucous in church history. In the end, the Council affirmed that Jesus has two natures joined in a "hypostatic" union. It also affirmed that Mary is the mother of God, the God-bearer (*Theotokos*).

Cyril of Alexandria (now Saint Cyril) presided at Ephesus—and with a heavy hand. He opened the Council before all the delegates had arrived, including Nestorius, patriarch of Constantinople, who had gained many supporters with his teaching that Mary is the mother of Jesus the man but not the mother of God. Even after all delegates had arrived from Rome and from the East, the teachings of Nestorius were discredited, and he was deposed as patriarch. Unable to accept the Council's rulings, he broke away and formed the Nestorian Church, which had adherents primarily in the East. Meanwhile, devotion to Mary flourished.

In proclaiming the word of God, priests now deliver a "homily," a reflection on the Scriptures as they apply to people's lives. Prior to the Council, the preaching of priests was often instructional, going through the Creed or Ten Commandments every few years. These "sermons" were not necessarily linked to the Scriptures. Also, since Vatican II, laypeople now proclaim the first two readings as a participation in our common priesthood arising from baptism.

As presider at Eucharist and the other sacraments, the priest is to lead the community to full, conscious, active participation. Previously, many who attended Mass felt like spectators. Now the priest leads the faith community to a meaningful participation in the life, death and resurrection of the Lord. The priest is called the "presider" to make it clear that the entire assembly is celebrating the sacraments according to their roles.

For centuries, the priest was the central authority in a community, the dominant figure in a parish. Prior to Vatican II there was no parish council to advise the priest in making decisions, no finance committee to monitor parish monies and no lay liturgical ministers. The priest also ran the entire educational effort of the parish.

Today many people participate in the administrative, educational and liturgical life of the parish. Collaboration is the key word. Appropriate sharing of authority and responsibility is essential.

This "working with" others is now a central characteristic of a good pastoral team and has affected the life of the priest in many ways. The priest must be willing to let go of some favorite ministries and to orchestrate the vast number of ministries necessary for healthy parish life.

Pastoral care, service to those in need, is an essential part of the priest's ministry. Here, too, things have changed. The priest is often unable to personally address all the concerns in the parish. Hands-on ministry is giving way to coordinating ministries in which others are trained and commissioned to offer pastoral care.

CHALLENGES OF OUR CULTURE

Ministry, be it that of priests, religious or laity, is done in a cultural context. Three factors deserve attention as we reflect on the ministry of the ordained.

Authority. People in authority have power. When someone is put in a position of leadership—a president, a principal, a parent, a priest—he or she must also be given the power to fulfill his or her responsibilities. Power can be used for self-serving interests or for servant-leadership. Priests are called to serve. If they use their authority for personal gain or abuse their power, they contradict their vocation.

Authority in the United States has fallen on hard times. Freedom has become the primary value, and few people are comfortable with the concept of submission. Authoritarian leadership will be rejected. Servant-leaders will be respected and followed.

Expectations. Prior to Vatican II priests were expected to provide the sacraments and be responsible administrators and caring pastors. Most of their time and energy was given to celebrating Mass, hearing confessions, visiting the sick, counseling those with problems and instructing people preparing for the sacraments. The expectations of priests have escalated. The priest must not only preach well but also be aware of and address social issues, reach out to the ecumenical community, lead a pastoral team, handle hiring and conflict resolution, show pastoral sensitivity, foster stewardship and a sense of mission—and more.

These many demands can lead to discouragement, anger and burnout. Having too many irons in the fire makes for an unbalanced life and can cause serious health problems—physical, psychological and spiritual. One of the challenges for priests today is to discern which expectations are realistic and appropriate, and which are neurotic and damaging.

One of the markings of holiness is humility. Everyone bumps up against limitations and weaknesses. Priests are not immune to this human condition. One cannot be "all things to all people." Today more than ever, priests should not be put in a position that will lead to failure. Clarification of roles and boundaries is extremely important.

Culture. Priests, like all people, are influenced by movies, television, the Internet, consumerism, violence and all the other societal forces that affect daily life. Some of these influences are healthy and life-giving, others are destructive and harmful. For good or ill, we breathe in the air of our culture. No one is exempt.

Never before has there been such a need for courageous, discerning hearts to keep the priest and his people grounded in gospel values—the dignity of the human person, the power of love and forgiveness, the need for compassion and courage, the presence of a God of mercy and love.

The Vatican II document, *The Church in the Modern World,* points out the need to integrate faith with the political, social, economic and cultural forces that impinge on our spiritual lives. Priests need a familiarity with social issues, political concerns, economic influences and cultural movements if they are to bring the gospel into contemporary life. In bringing the Good News to today's world, priests need a clear understanding of the signs of the times and how to adapt the message for various groups and elements of society.

GETTING PERSONAL

FATHER CYPRIAN DAVIS, O.S.B.

When Cyprian Davis became a Catholic at fifteen, he entered a church whose members included all racial and ethnic groups and nationalities. At least in theory, he and other blacks added a richness that was needed and welcomed by that universal church. But it took Vatican II and the influence of the 1960s civil-rights movement to nudge the church toward a genuine appreciation of the gift of blackness.

Today, Father Cyprian Davis, professor of church history at St. Meinrad School of Theology in Indiana, looks back in wonder at the changes he has witnessed. After he entered the Benedictines and was ordained, he earned a doctorate in history from the Catholic University of Louvain in Belgium. As he finished his studies, Vatican II was just getting underway. There was a buzz in the air about the changes the Council might bring.

When he returned to the U.S. in 1963, there was another kind of stirring: the civil-rights movement. He and fellow Benedictines attended Martin Luther King's "I Have a Dream" speech as part of the March on Washington. "We Catholics were present in full force," Father Davis said. "Our being there was right in tune with the notion of the Second Vatican Council that the church is to be involved in the problems of the day."

More important changes were to come, including new energy among black Catholics and liturgies reflecting black cultural heritage.

Father Davis credits Pope Paul VI with carrying Vatican II forward after the death of Pope John XXIII. "He implemented it, he fostered it."

FUTURE OF PRIESTLY MINISTRY

It has been nearly forty years since the last session of Vatican II. During that time tremendous changes have taken place in both the world and the life of the church. Our self-understanding as church and our sense of ministry have developed and been transformed. The revision of the sacraments, new emphasis on Scripture, deeper appreciation of Tradition, dialogue with world religions and cultures, and ecumenical activities have all affected the life of the ordained minister. Where are we now, and what does the future hold?

Shortage of priests. The response to the call to priesthood has dramatically declined in the Western world. Many dioceses are in crisis as they attempt to provide pastoral care. While the shortage has drawn more laypeople into ministry, parish sacramental needs remain urgent. Some priests are celebrating up to six Masses each weekend. Many priests are serving two, three, even four parishes and feel inadequate trying to provide comprehensive leadership. Seeking priests from other countries is one response to the shortage, but this has its limitations. The reduction in family size has shrunk the vocation pool, and the secularization of our society is an obstacle for many in hearing God's call. Yet, in all this, we know that God is calling.

Sexual abuse. The clergy sexual abuse crisis has done great harm to the victims of this crime as well as to the entire church. The problem is being addressed but the harm has been done, and it will take many years before trust is restored.

The whole culture is radically confused about the issue of sexuality. The current media, be it television, movies or the lifestyles portrayed, continue to give a distorted vision of God's great gift of human sexuality. Priests and all the people acutely need a reverent appreciation of this gift.

Friendship and community. Our social nature as humans demands healthy and wholesome relationships. Priests need affection and support, friends and community. Our American individualism has fostered a loneliness that affects all members of society. Good friendships are a tremendous grace. In friendship, joys and sorrows are shared and life is lived deeply. Community is at the heart of the church. To care for and share with one another, to serve the common good, is part of the work of the kingdom.

Spirituality. A petition from the Divine Office reads: "Lord Jesus, you are the true vine and we are the branches: allow us to remain in you, to bear much fruit, and to give glory to the Father." Drifting is one of the diseases of our age. Spirituality provides a center and an anchor. Priests need to ground their lives in prayer and ministry. Out of their dialogue with God, priests will be able to sustain a vision and offer people a perspective. By serving people with love and compassion they will build up the Body of Christ. Connected to the Lord through prayer and sacraments, their spiritual life will flourish, leading to service of people and the glory of God. Priests, acting in the name and person of Jesus, must maintain a deep relationship with the Lord if their ministry is to be fruitful and joyful.

IDENTITY AND MISSION

In Stephen Covey's popular book, *The Seven Habits of Highly Effective People*, the author suggests writing a mission statement before one attempts to live one's responsibilities. Vatican II was a mission statement process wherein the identity of the church and all its members—lay, religious and ordained—were given a vision of identity as well as mission. The sixteen documents are blueprints that we will do well to pray over as we journey together as the People of God. Priests, called to holiness and service, have a unique role to play in fostering the kingdom and giving God glory.

A NEW LANGUAGE

permanent diaconate: an ordained ministry of service with roots in the early church (Acts 6:1–7). Both single and married men can be ordained as permanent deacons to assist at Eucharist, bless marriages, proclaim the gospel, preach, preside at funerals and do works of charity. A single permanent deacon commits to celibacy. A married deacon vows not to remarry if his wife dies.

collegiality: a sharing of authority and responsibility between the pope and the world's bishops. Balanced decisions on important questions are possible because of the number of those giving input for the good of the universal church.

Questions for Discussion and Reflection

• The role of the priest is still changing as a result of Vatican II as well as the declining number of those responding to the call to priestly ministry. What changes have you experienced?

• Are the changes in the priesthood affecting your parish community in positive or negative ways? Some of both?

• How can you offer support to the priests you know and encourage young men to consider a priestly vocation?

CHAPTER SEVEN

Called to Holiness and Service: Lay Ministry

KAREN SUE SMITH

Since Vatican II the role of lay Catholics within the church community has changed markedly. Laypersons, who previously saw themselves as "less" than clergy and religious, are responding to the baptismal call to holiness and sharing their faith in both word and action.

As more individuals claim their rightful roles as members of the People of God, the church, and indeed the world, are being transformed.

Today, in parishes of all types and sizes, large numbers of lay Catholics serve as catechists and leaders of Bible study groups, small Christian communities and planning committees. Laypeople make up pastoral councils and finance committees, sponsor other adults through the rites of Christian initiation, and serve as music ministers, lectors, extraordinary ministers of Holy Communion, ushers and greeters at Sunday worship.

They play leading roles in Catholic institutions outside the parish, too—in dioceses and hospitals as well as schools, colleges and universities. All the while, most bear significant responsibilities at home, at work and in civic life. As baptized followers of Christ, lay Catholics are actively attempting to integrate their faith into all they do.

This all hardly sounds startling, especially to those too young to remember the church before Vatican II. In actuality, however, it represents an enormous turnabout in the self-understanding of Catholics. Before the Council, *none* of these activities were open to laypeople, and some of these roles didn't exist at all.

In the decades leading up to the Second Vatican Council, Catholics thought of the church as a pyramid. At the top was the pope, followed by cardinals, bishops, priests, and men and women religious. (There were no permanent deacons before Vatican II.) The bottom row was occupied by the laity.

The pyramid accurately depicted the hierarchical way in which the church was governed, but was often misinterpreted as if it showed rankings of Christian holiness as well. Not every pope had been declared a saint, and some laypersons actually had been, yet of all the saints the church had officially recognized throughout history, only a few laypersons had ever made the grade—and those who did tended to be martyrs or royalty. Holiness seemed to elude the laity as a whole.

THEN AND NOW
LATERAN COUNCIL IV (A.D. 1215)

The Fourth Lateran Council is often called "the Great Council." Pope Innocent III called large numbers of church leaders, the heads of religious orders and a number of secular rulers to gather in Rome in November 1215 to address a wide variety of issues facing the church at a time when Christianity was in decline. They dealt with their tasks in the space of only nineteen days.

Some of the Council's seventy decrees, offensive and embarrassing to modern-day readers, reflect a sense of threat from non-Christian religions, including Islam and Judaism. A period of preparation for the next Holy Land crusade was spelled out and a precise date set for its start. It did not come to pass, however, because of the unexpected death of Pope Innocent.

The churchmen at Lateran IV also addressed significant spiritual issues facing the church such as heresies and the lifestyle of the clergy. Turning their attention to the Eucharist, they used the word *transubstantiation* to describe the long-held belief that, at Mass, the bread and wine are changed into Jesus' body and blood. Finally, the Council ruled that all Christians are required to

> celebrate the sacrament of penance (if a mortal sin needs to be confessed) and of Eucharist at least once a year.

Catholic youngsters who appeared to take their faith seriously were nudged toward religious life or the priesthood. If celibate life was the highest calling, Catholics reasoned that married life must be second best. The laity's role of that era has been summed up in three verbs: "pray, pay and obey."

Laypersons were like fans who attend home games and cheer for the team. Parishioners worshiped every Sunday, made weekly confession, fasted on Fridays and sent their children to Catholic schools. The most pious joined parish societies (the Knights for men; sodalities for women). Laywomen washed and ironed the altar linens, but no layperson except an altar boy ever stepped beyond the altar rail. "Not feeling worthy" was a common expression in the years leading up to Vatican II.

A FLOOD OF OPPORTUNITIES

Gradually, as the teachings of Vatican II were made public, it became clear that not only the clergy and religious, but all Catholics are "called to holiness." The bishops taught: "All the faithful are invited and obliged to try to achieve the holiness and perfection of their own state of life" (*Dogmatic Constitution on the Church, Lumen Gentium,* 42). The laity had been invited to move out of the spectator section and become players. This was startlingly new.

Holiness is not primarily an individual undertaking, however. Christ calls "a people" (*Dogmatic Constitution on the Church,* 9) and incorporates them "into the church by baptism." All the baptized are "obliged both to spread and to defend the faith" as "true witnesses." Baptism binds us to Christ and to each other. Married couples, the bishops wrote, are to "help one another to attain holiness" and to educate their children in the faith through "word and example" (*Dogmatic Constitution on the Church,* 11). The Council documents describe the church as the entire community.

Whoever would follow Christ's example must be dedicated to his mission of healing, saving and transforming the world. As Jesus taught, compassion is key.

Millions of Catholics have not only heard this call to holiness, but also responded by volunteering for ministries most had never heard of before. Since the Council, lay involvement in parishes and at all levels of the church has flourished. What follow are just a few examples of the opportunities now available to lay Catholics.

Turning to Education

Many laypersons expressed a desire to learn more about Scripture and theology, promptly setting off a mini-boom in religious publishing and a bulge in enrollments at schools of theology. One unexpected result is that some thirty thousand laypersons, trained in pastoral ministry, are now employed in Catholic parishes. Roughly the same number are currently preparing for church service. These laypersons speak of having a "vocation" to church ministry.

Based on their experience in Christian living, millions of other laypeople regularly teach one another in parish faith-sharing groups, adult faith-formation programs and the adult initiation process (RCIA). In parochial schools and parish religious education, parents teach each other's children, since most catechists today are laypeople.

On the job, in lunchtime meetings and during informal conversations over coffee, Catholics around the nation explore the links between their faith and their work: How does one bring Catholic values into the workplace and into society at large? What does it mean to have a "vocation" as a teacher, lawyer, politician, firefighter or athlete? Regarding civic debate, lay Catholics take their role seriously, informing their consciences, forming their views and articulating their positions on war and peace, welfare, life issues and other important ethical questions.

Evangelization Starts at Home

The theology of the "domestic church" sketched in the documents of Vatican II looks on the Catholic home as the church in microcosm—a center of prayer, witness and service. Catholic parents bear primary responsibility for transmitting the faith to the next generation. Since they must be well-prepared for the task, parish formation and sacramental preparation programs are designed to assist them.

Some Catholics have even become foreign or home missionaries through lay missioner programs established by religious orders (such as the Franciscans, Jesuits and Sisters of Mercy) after Vatican II. Originally designed as short-term immersion experiences for single young adults, a few of these programs have expanded to include older adults, married couples, families with children and retirees.

Ministering to the Least

Catholic laypeople have become more service-conscious, seeing outreach to persons in need as an essential part of holiness. Most parishes sponsor social ministries, including those that promote justice, as a matter of course. Entrepreneurial Catholics have started their own organizations in fields as diverse as prisoner care and health care, food banks and job banks, responsible investing and micro-loans. Catholics support a vast array of such projects sponsored by the U.S. bishops' Catholic Campaign for Human Development and Catholic Relief Services, which works internationally to alleviate hunger, disease and human suffering.

CURRENT CHALLENGES

Given such rich opportunities for faith development and ministry, Catholics have begun to realize that the pyramid model of church no longer adequately represents the church they experience as the People of God. No other image, however, has yet replaced it in the Catholic imagination. Replacing this model and addressing the following challenges are some of our ongoing tasks.

Taking Responsibility for the Mission of the Church

It is easy to become overwhelmed by the pace and complexity of modern life and disappointed by the failures of our church. Yet if the church is truly the community of the baptized, then it will be strengthened as each Catholic matures. The task is to focus on the main goal: charity—love of God and neighbor. Holiness is only a byproduct.

As Catholics, we know that our spiritual life, while personal, is also corporate. It is up to us to become a people of deep prayer, our eyes open to the needs of the world around us. If, guided by the Holy Spirit and sustained by Christ's presence in the Eucharist, we can learn real compassion, then we will sustain one another. If we can learn to lead and not merely follow, we can more directly shape our church's future and further its mission to the world.

Engaging Lapsed and Passive Catholics

Nearly two-thirds of Catholics no longer attend Mass weekly. Many worship occasionally but do so as if still sitting in the bleachers or on the bench. The possible causes of this reality are many. What matters is that the church extend the invitation "to put on the mind of Christ" as baptized members of the People of God. Active Catholics must find ways to reach out to their inactive sisters and brothers. Catholics need to spell out for others how their faith contributes to major life choices, helps them at work and fosters their own community participation and spiritual growth.

Reaching Future Generations

Many young adult Catholics do not attend Mass or overtly practice Catholicism. They may subscribe to certain principles, such as caring for the downtrodden, but think of themselves more as "spiritual" than "religious." This separation from their roots occurs during some critical years—the period of dating, marriage and beginning a family. Since faith is passed on primarily from parent to child, the church stands to lose much whenever a young adult stops practicing the faith. Knowing how important married life and parenting are, the People of God need to extend special assistance and instruction to newlyweds, single parents and parents of young children.

Faith cannot be forced upon anyone, of course. We Catholics must do all we can to woo back our young. What can we offer them? We can offer genuine hospitality, dialogue, friendship, compassionate example and prayer that the Spirit will bring to fruition what was planted at baptism. We must also insist that our parishes provide quality liturgy and persuasive evangelization.

CONCLUSION

In the last fifty years our church has experienced euphoric highs, like Vatican II, when the Spirit seemed to be embodied in our pope and bishops as they reached out to the modern world. It has also experienced painful lows, like the recent revelations of scandal and poor leadership. What we learn from such experiences and how we grow as a church are our witness to the world and our legacy to future generations of the church.

GETTING PERSONAL
MEGEEN WHITE

Long before she'd even heard of Vatican II, Megeen White, now thirty-six, had the mission bug. Long before she read the Council's *Decree on the Church's Missionary Activity*, she wanted to build up God's kingdom—somewhere, somehow.

She caught the bug early, growing up in a family committed to faith, service and volunteering. As a teen she was haunted by images of the famine in Ethiopia and "wanted to give up everything for God" just as Saint Francis of Assisi had done. In college she prepared for a career in science but made sure to nourish herself with theology courses in case she decided to pursue ministry.

At age twenty-three Megeen discovered Franciscan Mission Service (FMS), based in Washington, D.C., and found her niche—a program for lay missionaries serving in overseas missions. She spent three years in Zimbabwe and Zambia serving as a high school science teacher, pastoral minister, Bible study coordinator, youth minister, catechist and outreach worker.

Today Megeen is codirector of FMS. She's quick to reminisce about her years in Africa: the "special joy" of working with young people and watching them "grow in their faith and as citizens," "listening to people's life stories," "living in the present moment," remembering "how much people gave and shared of the little they had" and recalling "deeply enriching friendships."

"Vatican II said we are all missionaries by our baptism," Megeen said. "God is calling each of us to live our lives and our faith in fullness. We are all chosen and sent."

A NEW LANGUAGE

theology of the laity: a term—dating to the 1950s, with roots in the theology of Cardinal John Henry Newman in the nineteenth century, and endorsed by Vatican II—affirming that the church consists of all baptized members. Through the power and gifts of the Holy Spirit, the laity share in the mission and ministry of the church.

priesthood of believers: the sharing of the faithful in Christ's mission as priest, prophet and king. Through baptism all believers are part of the common priesthood, joining in offering the Eucharist, receiving the sacraments, praying and living a holy life of self-denial and charity.

Questions for Discussion and Reflection

• What have you witnessed of the changing role of the laity since Vatican II? What has been your reaction to these changes? Your parish's reaction?

• If the pyramid model of church no longer fits the current experience of the People of God, what characteristics should the image or model have that replaces it?

• How well have you embraced your own baptismal call to holiness and service? What new opportunities for involvement might you consider pursuing in the future?

CHAPTER EIGHT
Marriage and Family Life: The Domestic Church
MARIE AND BRENNAN HILL

A look at our own parents offers a snapshot of Catholic marriage in the period before the Second Vatican Council. Marcelle and Bill (Marie's parents) were a traditional Catholic couple. They fell in love very young and were married before the high altar. They were encouraged to have all the children "that the Lord sent," thus welcoming seven and sending them all to Catholic schools. Harry and Elva (Brennan's parents) were Protestant and Catholic, respectively, and had what was called a "mixed marriage." They needed to get special permission to marry, and their ceremony had to be small and private. Harry, a Lutheran, had to promise that he would allow the children to be raised Catholic. The marriage ended in divorce. Elva was not able to get an annulment when she chose to remarry; she was excommunicated.

> The family is the most intimate experience of church, the place where love, forgiveness and trust should first be encountered.

The Catholic understanding of marriage in those days was largely in terms of its purposes. The primary purpose was the procreation and education of children. The secondary purpose was mutual help and as a remedy for sexual desire. The husband was seen as the head of the family while the woman was the heart. Marriage legitimized a couple's sexual pleasure.

Prior to Vatican II, there were some efforts to broaden the church's understanding of marriage. In 1930 Pope Pius XI wrote that the mutual love of husband and wife should have the prime place in marriage. In Europe some theologians proposed a more personal approach to marriage that emphasized human dignity and the centrality of married love. While these ideas did not immediately prevail, they did lay the foundation for the changes that officially came with the Second Vatican Council.

THEN AND NOW
CONSTANTINOPLE I (A.D. 381)

The 150 bishops who gathered for several months in Constantinople (now Istanbul) in the late fourth century were continuing the work begun at the Council of Nicaea some fifty years earlier. That council had condemned the heresy of Arianism, which denied the divinity of Jesus. But it inadvertently introduced new questions about the relationship of the three persons of the Trinity in the creed it developed.

Constantinople I again condemned Arianism, a heresy that long divided the church. The Council also reaffirmed the earlier creed (known as the Nicene Creed) and added the teaching that the Holy Spirit is one with God the Father and the Son. The bishops at Constantinople proclaimed their belief "in the Spirit...proceeding forth from the Father, co-worshipped and co-glorified with Father and Son." The Western church later added wording which stresses that the Spirit proceeds from the Son as well as the Father. The teaching on the Spirit developed at Constantinople I remains central to the creed we profess today.

Key roles at Constantinople were played by Saints Basil the Great, Gregory Nazianzen and Gregory of Nyssa. Meanwhile, Pope Damasus I was neither informed of nor invited to the Council.

THE CHURCH IN THE WORLD
The bishops of the Council treated the topic of marriage in the central document, the *Pastoral Constitution on the Church in the Modern World (Gaudium et Spes)*. This document was a direct response to Pope John XXIII's original vision for the Council—

that the church update itself and look to "the signs of the times" in carrying out its gospel mission.

The document opens with the now classic statement: "The joys and hopes, the grief and anguish of the people of our time, especially of those who are poor or afflicted, are the joys and hopes, the grief and anguish of the followers of Christ as well" (*Church in the Modern World*, 1). The church declared itself in solidarity with the people of the world and resolved to serve their needs, point to God's presence among us and read "the signs of the times" in the struggle for human dignity. Then the Council turned to the most basic unit of human society, the family, and observed that fostering healthy marriages and families is foundational to personal and social well-being.

THE PEOPLE OF GOD

Perhaps the most influential contribution of the Council was the description of the church as the "People of God." Previously the church had been largely identified with the clergy and men and women religious. Now all members could say, "We are church!" This was uniquely important for married people, for their state of life was traditionally viewed as being for those who did not have "vocations." Now, married life was being recognized as a genuine calling in its own right.

THE DOMESTIC CHURCH

The Council further recognized the dignity of marriage by declaring that families were genuinely "church." The Council restored the ancient concept of "domestic church" as it declared: "In what might be regarded as the domestic church, the parents are to be the first preachers of the faith for their children by word and example" (*Dogmatic Constitution on the Church, Lumen Gentium*, 11).

The early church began in house churches, where families were the heart of the communities and from which ministers were first called to use their personal gifts to serve the needs of the larger community. The family is the most intimate experience of church, the place where love, forgiveness and trust should first be encountered. This is the family church, whose members are called to embody Christ in everyday life.

MARRIAGE AS SACRAMENT

The Council moved from the older contractual view of the sacrament of marriage to one of *covenant*. God's covenant of love and fidelity to his people through Christ "now encounters Christian spouses through the Sacrament of Marriage" (*Church in the Modern World*, 48). This sacrament is uniquely a symbol, not through material things like oil, wine or water, but through two persons joining their lives in love and in faith in Christ. The couple, the true "ministers" of the sacrament, are now a sign of the real presence of Jesus in the world.

The sacramental theology of marriage has continued to deepen, especially now that married people themselves often develop this theology. Marriage is understood more as a dynamic symbol of Christ's power in marriage, a reality that only begins at the ceremony and then must be nurtured and strengthened throughout the marriage. Marriages develop, deepen and grow or they weaken, wither and even die.

The importance of commitment to the things that really matter is evident. In our busy, materialistic and throwaway era when the permanence and fidelity of marriage are threatened, more couples realize that they must regularly focus attention on the center of it all: their relationship. Couples committed to sacramental marriage realize that if their lives are to be rooted in the Lord, they need a deep spirituality and a commitment to prayer.

THE PASTORAL CARE OF MARRIAGE

The deepening theology of marriage has brought about new ministries. Programs are provided by married couples to prepare the engaged for marriage, retreats and evening programs help couples strengthen their marriages, and diocesan offices offer services and counseling to couples and families.

Movements such as Worldwide Marriage Encounter and Retrouvaille (for troubled marriages) have provided inspiration and resources to couples since the Council. Such programs help husbands and wives with their communication skills and suggest ways to strengthen the marriage relationship.

PARTNERSHIP

Vatican II's emphasis on personal dignity and social rights seems to have contributed to more egalitarian models of marriage. In a growing number of marriages today spouses choose to be equal partners, sharing decision-making, lifestyle choices, household tasks and parenting responsibilities.

Since the Council more women have found their voices both in the church and in the home. They have become more independent and career-oriented and thus call upon their husbands to do more of the child care and household tasks. This model, of course, requires much more consultation, compromise and flexibility.

Ideally, friendship is also part of the marriage partnership. Many husbands and wives view their mates as their best friend as well as their spouse. This dimension of the relationship usually calls for even deeper levels of intimacy and sharing. Jesus once told his followers that he did not call them servants, but friends (John 15:15). Many Christian couples have reclaimed this aspect of relationship since Vatican II.

COUPLE POWER

The Council called all Christians to holiness and ministry. Married couples have responded with a deep spirituality and commitment to service, discovering a new "couple power" in ministry. We have witnessed married couples working in homeless shelters and soup kitchens, demonstrating in peace marches and advocating for the poor at city hall with unique power and influence. We have met "lifer" couples in El Salvador and Nicaragua, who live with the poor and who give their lives in quiet service. Many couples have uniquely taken to heart the church's commitment to solidarity with the poor of the world.

OTHER CHURCHES AND RELIGIONS

Pope John XXIII's vision for the Second Vatican Council included concern for Christian unity and respect for other religions. The Council acknowledged that God's plan of salvation includes all who sincerely seek God. The Council also encouraged respectful dialogue with other churches and religions and developed new procedures for ecumenical and interfaith marriages.

Before the Council Catholics were strongly discouraged from marrying "outside the church." At present, over 50 percent of Catholics in the U.S. choose to marry someone who is not a Catholic. These marriages now can be held in the sanctuary in the presence of ministers from both faiths. Moreover, the spouse from the other faith is no longer required to promise to allow the children to be raised Catholic. Instead, the Catholic spouse promises to do all in his or her power to raise the children Catholic. In addition, both spouses are encouraged to learn about each other's religious beliefs and practices.

GETTING PERSONAL

SISTER ANGELA ANN ZUKOWSKI, M.H.S.H.

Many see Jesus as the perfect communicator. But the church he founded still struggles to communicate effectively. Even the Fathers at Vatican II found it daunting to tackle the issue: Their *Decree on the Mass Media (Inter Mirifica)* is considered by most commentators to be the weakest document the Council produced.

Sister Angela Ann Zukowski, a Mission Helper of the Sacred Heart and one of the church's leading experts in communications, sees the Vatican II decree as a lost opportunity. But she has spent more than thirty years moving the church forward by helping to produce new church documents on communication and in her work in cable TV, radio, satellite and the newest kid on the block— the World Wide Web.

She is guided by two questions: What did Jesus say and do? What can we learn from Jesus as a communicator?

Sister Angela Ann, director of the Institute for Pastoral Initiatives at the University of Dayton (UD), sees great potential for the church to express itself in our culture. The printed word will always be very important, she said, but "the Internet is the place where all will converge. The Web is so woven into the fabric of our culture. We don't want to lose this new tool. That's where the dialogue is taking place."

Some focus on the Web's dangers; Sister Angela Ann sees its potential. UD offers dozens of online courses in adult faith formation for catechists and lay ministers. The potential of the Internet is unknowable, she says. The only sure thing is that "what we see now is just the tip of the iceberg."

DIVORCE AND REMARRIAGE

For nearly a century, the church forbade divorce and remarriage, and any Catholic who divorced and remarried in the U.S. was excommunicated. Pope John XXIII's plea for mercy rather than punishment led to changes in both attitudes and procedures. Grounds for annulment were reexamined in light of the interpersonal dimension of marriage acknowledged by Vatican II. (A declaration of nullity, commonly referred to as an annulment, is the church's official ruling that a sacramental marriage never existed and that the persons involved are now free to marry again.) In 1977 the excommunication ruling was lifted at the petition of the U.S. bishops to Pope Paul VI.

Nevertheless, the majority of Catholics who divorce don't seek annulments. This has created a significant pastoral problem for the church. Still, the church has made strides in ministering to its divorced members. In his 1981 apostolic exhortation on *The Role of the Christian Family in the Modern World (Familiaris Consortio)*, Pope John Paul II noted that the church "cannot abandon" Catholics who have divorced and remarried. "I earnestly call upon pastors and the whole community of the faithful to help the divorced, and...make sure that they do not consider themselves as separated from the church.... Let the church pray for them, encourage them and show herself a merciful mother, and thus sustain them in faith and hope" (84).

ONGOING ISSUES

Family planning has created a particular dilemma for the church. The Vatican has taken a firm stand in opposition to artificial birth control, and many Catholic couples find themselves in conflict with the church's position.

A NEW LANGUAGE

domestic church: a term used in the Council document *Lumen Gentium* to refer to the family. Within the domestic church, parents "are to be the first preachers of the faith for their children by word and example" (*Lumen Gentium*, 11).

vocation: a call from God to a particular state of life through which the person strives for holiness. The Second Vatican Council made it clear that there is a "universal call to holiness" in the church that extends to all the faithful (*Lumen Gentium*, 39).

This and many other questions concerning marriage and family life will no doubt receive serious attention as the church continues to meet Good Pope John's challenge to read and respond to "the signs of the times."

Questions for Discussion and Reflection

• How do the different marriages you see around you reflect the church's changing and growing understanding of the sacrament of matrimony?

• How well does your parish support marriage and family life? How does it support separated and divorced people? The widowed? Singles? What more can be done?

• What are the "signs of the times" telling you to do to strengthen your own marriage or another significant family relationship?

CHAPTER NINE
Today's Church: A Look in the Mirror
WILLIAM H. SHANNON

What does the church have to say about the death penalty? What is church teaching on gay marriage? What position does the church take on optional celibacy for priests? In the context of these questions, I want to put a different question to the reader: What reality does the word *church* in such statements immediately bring to mind for you? When you hear the word *church*, does it mean the pope and his Vatican officials? Or do you think of the bishop and his diocesan staff? Or perhaps *church* brings to mind your local pastor and the various ministers in your parish community.

All the baptized are the People of God. All are called to build up the church: the members of the hierarchy in their way, and the rest of the baptized in theirs.

A FOURTH WAY OF THINKING "CHURCH"
Is there another way of thinking about church? Would it occur to you to put the question this way: What do *I* think about these issues? What do *my fellow parishioners* think about them? What do *Catholic people throughout the world* think about them? Are these also viable ways of understanding church?

It is probably true to say that before the Second Vatican Council most people would have been satisfied to accept the first three ways of thinking about church as adequate descriptions. These views represent a hierarchical way of seeing church, a top-to-bottom view. What was revealed at the Council was a new vision of church. At least it was new to most people at the time. It actually goes back to a very early, biblical perspective.

THEN AND NOW
BASEL-FERRARA-FLORENCE-ROME (1431–1445)
It took several cities, two countries, a number of popes, one antipope and many years before the

work of the Council of Basel-Ferrara-Florence-Rome ended. Even then, many of its agreements and conclusions were never put into effect. A tug-of-war arose early and resurfaced regularly between Pope Eugene IV and the sparse number of bishops at Basel, Switzerland, who insisted on the superiority of their authority as members of a general church council (conciliarism) over that of any pope.

Both sides battled over who was better prepared to deal with the real item of business: ending the schism between the Eastern and Western churches. The location of the Council had political meaning for the two camps. Pope Eugene scored points for the papacy when he succeeded in moving the Council to Italy—first to Ferrara and then on to Florence and Rome. Meanwhile, a disgruntled, anti-papal faction continued to meet in Basel even after its members were excommunicated.

The serious theological and liturgical issues that confronted the Council were settled by pragmatic compromises that did not last. The promised union of East and West did not come to pass. One clear outcome of the Council was the demise of conciliarism.

VATICAN II'S VISION OF CHURCH

Fundamental to Vatican II's vision is an emphasis on the church as the People of God. True, the church is a hierarchical community. Note, though, that hierarchical is the adjective; community is the noun. Since nouns are more substantive than adjectives, it is fair to say that community trumps hierarchy. While hierarchy is important, the community must come first.

Preceding any distinction between lay and ordained is the reality of Christian baptism. Baptism incorporates us all into an egalitarian community in which all are one and equal in Christ. A priest, bishop or pope receives his Christian identity in the same way as all God's people: through baptism. As Cardinal Suenens said in a homily at a memorial Mass for Pope John XXIII, the most significant day in the life of a priest, bishop or pope is not the day of his ordination but the day he was baptized into Christ Jesus.

Yves Congar, one of the theologians of the Council, wrote that it is not laypersons who have to define themselves in terms of their relation to the hierarchy but rather the hierarchy that needs to define itself in relation to the whole People of God. It is most importantly the People of God of whom they are a part and whom they are called upon to serve.

All the baptized are the People of God. All are called to build up the church: the members of the hierarchy in their way, and the rest of the baptized in theirs. Giving priority to people fits well with the derivation of the word used for *church* in the New Testament. The Greek word for church is *ekklesia*. Its literal meaning is "those who are called together by God."

CHURCH BUILDINGS

Catholic church buildings may be called "churches" only in a derivative sense: They are not the church, but the place where the church, God's people, gather. In ancient times a pagan temple was the house of a particular god. The priest alone entered the temple; people prayed outside. The same was true of the Jewish temple in Jerusalem: It was the house of God. People gathered in courts outside the temple, and only the priest was allowed to enter it.

A Catholic church is very different. It is not God's house; it is rather the place where God's people assemble. You don't need a building to have the church. It is people, not bricks and mortar, that make up the church.

RETURN TO A COLLEGIAL MODEL

The Council also set out to decentralize the church. It did this by emphasizing the unique importance of each local church. It made clear that each bishop is the vicar of Christ in the local church over which he presides: "The bishops, as vicars and legates of Christ, govern by their counsels, persuasion and example the particular churches assigned to them" (*Dogmatic Constitution on the Church, Lumen Gentium,* 27). The local bishop, therefore, is not primarily an agent of Rome but of the Holy Spirit.

This shift in focus meant a return to the principle of collegiality—so important in the first millennium of Christianity. Collegiality means that the Catholic bishops throughout the world, together with and under the leadership of the pope, possess supreme authority and pastoral responsibility for the whole church. Besides the responsibilities they have in their local churches, bishops are called to have concern for the universal church.

The First Vatican Council asserted that the pope was able to exercise supreme authority without consulting the bishops. The Second Vatican Council, without denying that the pope can exercise such authority, suggested—at least hinted—that perhaps he ought not to do so. Before making any major statements, the pope would be well advised to consult with the bishops of the world so that what the Spirit is saying to the local churches can be incorporated into statements intended for the entire world.

The Book of Revelation offers sound advice in this regard. In the letters addressed to the local churches in Asia, each concludes with a similar message: *"Let anyone who has an ear listen to what the Spirit is saying to the churches"* (Revelation 2:7; emphasis added).

LOCAL COLLEGIALITY
But collegiality need not stop with the college of bishops. This principle needs to be extended to the local church. If the bishop wants to be a good teacher whose teaching reaches the minds and hearts of his people, he must also be a good listener.

He needs to hear what priests, religious and laity in his diocese are saying as they attempt to live out the gospel in their daily lives. When the bishop listens to them and incorporates their experiences into the teaching of the gospel, he will be better assured that his teaching will be vital as well as relevant.

The principle of collegiality deserves an even wider application. It should also find expression in the lives of the individual parishes in a diocese. After all, it is in their parish community that most Catholics experience the reality of church. It is here that they are baptized, confirmed and celebrate the Eucharist. It is the place where they marry and where their children are baptized. It is with their fellow parishioners and their pastors that they share the joys and sorrows, the agonies and the ecstasies of life.

Pastors of parishes need to listen to the faithful in their parish: "The sacred pastors...should recognize and promote the dignity and responsibility of the laity in the church. They should willingly use their prudent advice and confidently assign offices to them in the service of the church, leaving them freedom and scope for activity. Indeed, they should encourage them to take on work on their own initiative" (*Dogmatic Constitution on the Church*, 37).

This should be especially true in areas where the laity have expertise that their pastors lack. "To the extent of their knowledge, competence or authority, the laity are entitled, and indeed sometimes duty-bound, to express their opinion on matters which concern the good of the church" (*Dogmatic Constitution on the Church*, 37).

OTHER ECCLESIAL COMMUNITIES

There is an intriguing sentence in Vatican II's document on the church: "This church, constituted and organized as a society in the present world, *subsists* in the Catholic church" (*Dogmatic Constitution on the Church*, 8; emphasis added). If the Council Fathers who wrote this document had intended to say that the Christian church is *identical with* the Catholic church, they could have said so. The fact is that they chose not to say this; instead they picked a word that may be read to mean that perhaps the church of Christ extends beyond the boundaries of the Catholic church.

The Council even "hints" (I use the word "hints" advisedly) that it may be possible to extend the understanding of church beyond the Catholic church. The document on the church says: "The church has many reasons for knowing that it is joined to the baptized who are honored by the name of Christian, but do not profess the faith in its entirety or have not preserved unity of communion under the successor of Peter" (*Dogmatic Constitution on the Church,* 15). Such groups are described as "churches" or "ecclesiastical communities."

It is worth noting that, while Sacred Scripture has always been an important part of our Christian heritage, it has only been since the Council that the Catholic church has given due emphasis to it. Until then other Christian "ecclesiastical communities" were much more devoted to the Scriptures than were Catholics.

GETTING PERSONAL
DR. MARTIN MARTY

Drawing on an inquisitive mind, an outgoing personality and a press pass, Martin Marty made himself at home at the third session of Vatican II. Never mind that the Lutheran minister was attending the Council as associate editor at *Christian Century,* a Protestant magazine that once viewed the Catholic church with suspicion. It was the autumn of 1964, and Dr. Marty was in Rome to get a firsthand look at "the new world" that Pope John XXIII had set out to create.

It was a happy coincidence that Martin Marty bore the same name as the first bishop of St. Cloud, Minnesota, and hit it off with that bishop's successor. Thanks to him, Dr. Marty, initially restricted to English-speaking press conferences, suddenly had entrée to the Council sessions and to key players. "There were no limits to my access," he said. He enjoyed "moseying around" and getting closer to the workings of Catholicism than "a Protestant from Chicago" ever could have imagined.

His days began with worship. Evenings often included late-night dinners and discussions with bishops from around the world as well as up-and-coming theologians attending the Council. Dr. Marty took it all in with enthusiasm—and with gusto, gaining seventeen pounds during his three months in Rome!

Now a professor emeritus at the University of Chicago, where he taught for many years, Dr. Marty relishes the ecumenical breakthroughs made possible by Vatican II. But he harbors one "great frustration: that we Christians don't share communion at the altar."

INFALLIBILITY

The Second Vatican Council repeats the teachings of Vatican I on the infallibility, under certain specified conditions, of the college of bishops with the pope or of the pope alone without that college. However, Vatican II adds significantly to our understanding of the church's infallibility.

It points out that the People of God share in Christ's prophetic office. For this reason "the whole body of the faithful who have received an anointing which comes from the Holy One (see 1 John 2:20 and 27) cannot be mistaken in belief. It shows this characteristic through the entire people's supernatural sense of the faith, when 'from the bishops to the last of the faithful,' it manifests a universal consensus in matters of faith and morals" (*Dogmatic Constitution on the Church*, 12).

IS THE VISION OF VATICAN II FADING?

I have tried to describe the vision of church that emerged from Vatican II. We have to ask today, humbly but honestly: Is the vision of the Council being brought to fruition? Is the church becoming the church envisioned by the Council? Many would answer with a hesitant and regretful "no" or at least "not anywhere near what it should be."

Surely much has changed in the forty years since Vatican II. Laypeople are more and more involved in the life of the church.

This is a gain that can never be set back. Yet one cannot help but note the appearance of a strong current of thought and action aimed at gradually recentralizing the church. More and more authority is being withdrawn from local churches and concentrated in Rome. As one theologian described the way in which things seem to be moving: "The pope is no longer the *ultimate* authority; he is the *only* authority."

A NEW LANGUAGE

sense of the faithful (sensus fidelium): a phrase that refers to the church's infallibility of belief based on Christ sharing his prophetic office with the People of God. The church's teachings emerge from the faith of all its members, and "the whole body of the faithful...cannot be mistaken in belief" (*Dogmatic Constitution on the Church,* 12).

inculturation: the appropriate adaptation of the Catholic liturgy and institutions to the culture, language and customs of a people among whom the gospel is proclaimed. The church can "enter into communion with different forms of culture, thereby enriching both itself and the cultures themselves" (*Gaudium et Spes,* 58).

Still, the vision of the Council is there, calling us to become the church that it had hoped would come into being. Laypeople have an important role to play in preserving this vision and moving it forward to fulfillment.

Questions for Discussion and Reflection

• What does the word *church* mean to you? Has your perspective changed with the reading of this chapter? If so, how?

• How well is the principle of collegiality being modeled in your local church—by your bishop? By your pastor? How open and prepared is your community to accept the responsibilities that come with true collegiality?

• Father Shannon concludes this chapter by stating that laypeople have an important role in moving forward the Vatican II vision of church. What are you doing to preserve and promote this vision?

CHAPTER TEN
Our Church: Called to Be a Sign of Joy and Hope
WILLIAM H. SHANNON

On December 7, 1965, the Second Vatican Council, in its final session, adopted the *Pastoral Constitution on the Church in the Modern World*. Its tone and direction differed significantly from the other major documents of Vatican II. In them, the church had turned inward to shed the light of the gospel on itself to see what God willed it to be. In this new document the church looked outward to discover its role in today's world: a world of which it is, after all, a part, but a world that in many ways had ceased to take it seriously.

The church has a message for the modern world, as well as a listening ear and a cooperating heart.

PARTNERING WITH THE WORLD
The church not only looked outward; it did so in a way that no previous church council had ever done. It looked at the world and smiled, just as God must have smiled when he gazed on the world he had created and saw that it was very good. By contrast, other church councils had looked at the world and ignored it or deplored it, seeing it as a place of sin and corruption that they felt compelled to condemn.

Vatican II abandoned this negative mentality about the world outside of the church: It took the world to its heart in a spirit of concern and compassion. It would partner with the world in discerning "the true signs of God's presence and purpose in the events, needs and the desires which it shares with the rest of humanity today" (11).

A persistently positive attitude toward that world and an earnest desire to enter into dialogue with it make this document unique in the history of Council documents. Its title, "Joy and Hope" (in Latin, *Gaudium et Spes*), and its opening sentence give definite expression to the direction it took and the tone it adopted: "The joys and hopes, the grief and anguish of the people of our time, especially of those who are poor or afflicted, are the joys and hopes, the grief and anguish of the followers of Christ as well. Nothing that is genuinely human fails to find an echo in their hearts" (1).

THEN AND NOW
THE COUNCIL OF TRENT (1545–1563)

As the Council of Trent opened, the Protestant Reformation was in full swing. With one eye focused on addressing the questions that Martin Luther and other Protestants were raising and the other on confronting problems left untended for decades, the Fathers of the Council set out to clarify and correct, refute and reform.

The council that met at Trent in northeast Italy had two false starts, went through several interruptions (one a decade long) and required twenty-five sessions before it concluded. But, in the end, its decrees shaped the church up to the Second Vatican Council four hundred years later.

The Council of Trent stressed the importance of Scripture and Tradition and the office of the bishop. It called for professional training of priests in modern seminaries. It clarified the number and meaning of the sacraments, with special focus on original sin and baptism and the Real Presence of Christ in the Eucharist. It insisted on the importance of good works as well as faith. It attempted reform of almost every aspect of church life. When the Council of Trent ended, the church had a new catechism, a reformed Roman Missal and an index of forbidden books. Church doctrine had been made clearer, but Protestantism continued to grow.

WITNESSING IN THE HERE AND NOW

To identify what is "genuinely human" in today's world and to discern the church's role in supporting it are tasks that are essentially incarnational. The Incarnation means that Christ did not redeem the world from afar, but by involving himself in the human situation and becoming one of us. This incarnational principle was embraced at the Council and gave birth to a new understanding of the church's mission.

Before the Council, its mission focused almost exclusively on the "other world" and on assisting individuals to attain eternal salvation. *Gaudium et Spes* moved Catholics toward a new way of thinking that saw the church's mission as witnessing also to the love and compassion of God in the here and now. Divine love and compassion call us to work for justice, peace and healing in our globalized world.

The church has a message for the modern world, but also a listening ear and a cooperating heart. It seeks to keep abreast of the changes that are taking place so rapidly in today's world as the human race moves from a more static view of reality to a more dynamic and evolutionary one (5).

EMBRACING OUR DIGNITY

Gaudium et Spes, the Council's longest document, is in two parts. The first develops its teaching about the vocation of human beings, the world in which they carry it out and the church's role in helping people live it in today's world. Its four chapters deal with our dignity as human persons, the human community, humanity's activity in the universe and the role of the church in the modern world.

The second part focuses on questions and problems of special importance in today's world. Its five chapters deal with the dignity of marriage and the family; the development of culture; economic and social life; the political community; and fostering peace and establishing a community of nations.

Our dignity as humans flows from our creation in the image of God and our call to nothing less than communion with God.

The human response to God's call, though personal, is not solitary. Never before in history has it been more urgent to recognize the interdependence of the peoples of the world. Astounding advances in the empirical sciences, in technology and in the liberal arts have accumulated a vast fund of knowledge.

SEEKING WISDOM

The Council reminds us that the present age, more than any other, requires wisdom that can process knowledge and enable us to see that there are radical realities and deep human values that go beyond the immediate, the passing, the superficial. Wisdom helps us to grasp God's providence at work in human history, guiding that history to a fulfillment beyond mere human efforts.

The world's future depends on people endowed with such wisdom. In a significant contrast between the nations of wealth and power and the developing nations, the document states: "It should be pointed out that many nations which are poorer as far as material goods are concerned, yet richer in wisdom, can be of the greatest advantage to others" (15).

At the same time, the Council makes clear its belief in the goodness of human activity in the world. "Far from thinking that what human enterprise and ability have achieved is opposed to God's power as if the rational creature is a rival of the creator, Christians are convinced that the achievements of the human race are a sign of God's greatness and the fulfillment of his mysterious design" (34).

Great progress requires great vigilance. As our power increases, so does our responsibility as individuals and as members of the human community. It should be clear, therefore, that the gospel does not inhibit us from doing all we can for the genuine progress of the human race. On the contrary, it obliges us more strictly to work for everything that contributes in an authentic way to the greater good of humanity.

GETTING PERSONAL
FATHER MICHAEL JONCAS

Most of us, if asked, would easily be able to hum a few bars of "On Eagle's Wings." It has become one of the most familiar and popular songs sung in churches around the world—literally. It has been translated into Spanish, Vietnamese, Italian and Polish.

Its composer, Father Michael Joncas, fell in love with music as a child growing up in Minnesota. He was born there in 1951 into a family immersed in the performing arts. By the end of high school, Michael had taught himself the piano and twice won the statewide young composers' competition. After high school came seminary studies and his 1980 ordination as a priest of the Archdiocese of St. Paul-Minneapolis.

Today he plays keyboard, guitar and flute "adequately." He also claims more than two hundred pieces of liturgical music and fifteen collections of his compositions. But he has no favorites. "So much depends on the context in which the piece was written and performed. In some ways my 'favorite' composition is the next one I'm working on," he said.

Now a theology professor at the University of St. Thomas in St. Paul, Father Joncas is associated with post-Vatican II sacred music. But he agrees with the Council Fathers that the church's "treasury of sacred music" should be preserved. That includes "the particular glory of the Roman rite—Gregorian chant. My concern is only that any pre-Vatican II music used as part of the reformed liturgy be experienced as living prayer and not a museum piece."

RESPONDING TO FREEDOM

Human freedom is a wonderful manifestation of the divine image. *Gaudium et Spes*, in its remarkable tribute to human freedom (17), offers a vision unmatched by any previous council. Yet it does not ignore the fact that humans are wounded by sin and need God's grace to orient their freedom toward God.

One of the graces God gives us to guide our freedom is conscience. Conscience, we are told, is "the most secret core and sanctuary of the human person. There they are alone with God whose voice echoes in their depths. By conscience, in a wonderful way, that law is made known which is fulfilled in the love of God and of one's neighbor" (16). Our responsibility to form a correct conscience is something we can hardly achieve without the help of God's grace.

In discussing the existence of atheism in today's world, *Gaudium et Spes* shows a sympathetic understanding of people who espouse it, even suggesting that religious people bear some responsibility for its existence. Poorly instructed Christians may give false impressions of what Christian faith actually teaches about God. The god atheists reject may well be a god that a properly educated Christian would also reject. Likewise, the failure of Christians to live what they say they believe can quickly dry up any interest an atheist might have in learning about the God whom Christians say they worship, but whom they belie by their actions (19).

SHARING GIFTS

The laity, as citizens of the world, are especially empowered to bring the Christian message into the marketplace. As an earlier document, the *Dogmatic Constitution on the Church*, said, the laity have the right—even at times the duty—to make known, in areas of their own competence, their opinions on matters which concern the good of the church.

Part two of *Gaudium et Spes* begins with a section on marriage and the family. Avoiding older terminology that spoke of the primary and secondary purposes of marriage, it insists on the importance of conjugal love. "By its very nature the institution of marriage and married love are ordered to the procreation and education of the offspring and it is in them that it finds its crowning glory" (48). While avoiding the issue of contraception (reserved by Pope Paul VI to a special commission outside the Council), the Council spoke of the importance of responsible parenthood as a decision that married couples—with a properly formed conscience and with due attention to the teaching of the church—must make in terms of their own good and that of their children (50).

The articles on socioeconomic life echo and develop many of the themes contained in the social encyclicals of the popes from Leo XIII to Paul VI. While space prohibits detailed discussion, one overarching theme is clear: the growing concern about the inequalities between the advanced nations and the developing ones (63).

Several articles are devoted to the promotion of peace and the elimination, or at least the controlling, of the ravages of war. Peace is not just the absence of war: It is the work of justice. The proliferation of terribly destructive weaponry forces us "to undertake a completely fresh appraisal of war" (80).

The Council adopted the teaching of recent popes in condemning total war and the arms race, though allowing for limited wars of defense, as long as there is no competent international authority with appropriate powers to safeguard peace. It defends the right of conscientious objection to war and praises those who commit themselves to nonviolence. It calls us to join with all peace-loving people in pleading for peace and trying to achieve it (78).

A NEW LANGUAGE

evangelization: sharing the gospel through word and action in order to bring others to Christ. Evangelization includes internal conversion to Christ that affects not only individuals but also the culture. The desired result is that the culture and its institutions are changed to make them Christian and Catholic.

incarnational theology: through the birth of Jesus, the Incarnation, God made this earth his home. The whole world was blessed and all human flesh took on a new dignity.

STANDING AS A BEACON OF LIGHT

Gaudium et Spes concludes with a stirring call to all people who love the truth, whatever their culture, race or religion, to join together "to fashion a world better suited to the surpassing dignity of humanity, to strive for a more deeply rooted sense of universal sisterhood and brotherhood, and to meet the pressing appeals of our times with a generous and common effort of love" (91).

Gaudium et Spes was written at the time when the world's peace and security were threatened by the Cold War. Our world today must deal with a deadly terrorism that is often faceless and that may strike anywhere at any time. In such a situation the gospel message impels us to put forth every effort to work with people of good will to eliminate conditions that make for terrorism and to work for peace based on justice and freedom.

The church—confident in the assurance of the Lord Jesus to be with us at all times, even the darkest and seemingly hopeless times—stands as a beacon of light and hope in an otherwise darkening world. *Gaudium et Spes* supports that beacon of light. Its hopes are rooted in the goodness of God, surely, but also in the radical goodness of humanity.

Questions for Discussion and Reflection

• In what practical ways is the Catholic church a sign of joy and hope in the world today?

• Is your parish living out its mission to be a beacon of light and hope for its members? For citizens of the larger community? What more can be done?

• How well does the positive attitude toward the world so prevalent in *Gaudium et Spes* match your own? What fears or prejudices do you still need to dispel?

CHAPTER ELEVEN
Sharing Our Heritage of Faith
JOHN ROBERTO

We live in times of exciting developments in faith formation in the church. Parishes are engaged in new ways of encouraging Catholics of all ages to deepen their relationship with Christ and their understanding and practice of the faith.

> We need to encourage our parish communities to provide resources, programs, small groups and activities to nurture faith growth from birth through the later years of life.

Over the past forty years we have seen the reintroduction of the *Rite of Christian Initiation of Adults* as well as the growth of religious education programs for children and teens, family-centered religious education, youth ministry, parish renewal programs, adult faith formation, small faith-sharing groups and Bible studies to name only a few. Many of these are so commonplace we don't realize that they were absent from parish life prior to the Second Vatican Council and, in large part, were initiated in response to the vision and energy generated by it.

We also live in times that present tremendous new challenges for developing a Catholic way of life and sharing our faith with future generations. American Catholics have experienced the gradual loss of a distinctive Catholic culture. We are challenged by declining levels of participation among Catholics in parish life and, in particular, the Sunday assembly, resulting in fewer opportunities for people to experience the Catholic way of life and make it their own.

We are challenged in our families to find meaningful ways to create patterns of family faith sharing—learning, praying, celebrating, serving—that are woven into the fabric of daily life. Many of the challenges we face—individually and as parish communities—can be summarized in a question: How can we create a faith community in the parish and home that provides an ongoing support system for the development of a Catholic way of life?

THEN AND NOW
COUNCIL OF VIENNE (1311–1312)

The word *scandalous* has been used to describe the Council of Vienne. It was called by a timid pope, Clement V, in response to pressure from King Philip IV of France.

Philip was determined to be rid of the Knights Templar, a religious order of monk-knights originally founded to protect and guide pilgrims to the Holy Land. Riddled with debt and threatened by the Templars' power and wealth in France, Philip turned to a weakened pope to help him do his bidding. After Jerusalem fell to the Muslims in 1187 and Christians were ousted, the king had a perfect opening. He organized a propaganda campaign against the Templars by playing up rumors of heresy, shady business practices and secret rituals, and pressed Pope Clement for an official investigation. Before the Council of Vienne had opened, Philip had the Knights Templar arrested in France, appropriated their property and used torture to extract confessions of guilt.

The bishops at Vienne voted against abolishing the Templars, insisting the charges against them were unproven. Pope Clement, who owed his election to King Philip, overruled the bishops. He dissolved the group and ordered it out of existence. At King Philip's command, a number of its members were burned at the stake.

THE "OLD DAYS"

I went to public elementary school, so I was a "CCD kid." On Mondays I was released from school one hour early and took the public bus across town to Holy Rosary (Italian) Church. (What did you expect from someone named Roberto?) The sisters came over from the Catholic school and taught us in the church. Monday's program was for fifth through eighth graders, all together. Our textbook was the *Baltimore Catechism—Third Edition* (blue cover).

The sisters' teaching approach was pretty simple: Each week we would cover a series of questions. We responded from memory or by reading the answer from the book, and then they explained what it meant. By the end of the year we had covered all the questions and answers. When we came back the next year, we started all over again with the first question!

The catechism approach to faith formation reflected a static view of the Catholic faith and of learning. We were taught as children what we must believe and that we were to believe this for the rest of our lives. Once we had learned this as children, there was only a need for reminders and reinforcement through the rest of life. This usually happened through Sunday sermons, devotions and special missions.

Fortunately, my own faith formation was much more than CCD classes. I grew up in a three-generation, Italian-Catholic household. We actively participated in all aspects of parish life: the sacraments, feasts and festivals, traditions and social activities. I was surrounded by a Catholic support system of family, parish and friends.

FROM STATIC TO DYNAMIC

The Second Vatican Council replaced the static view of the Catholic faith with a more dynamic understanding. The church—and faith formation—were re-centered on the Gospels and the life, death and resurrection of Jesus Christ; on the sacraments, especially the Eucharist; and on service to the world.

The new terms "People of God" and "Pilgrim church" communicated the dynamism of this new approach in several important ways: (1) We learn throughout life. We never arrive; we are on a journey. (2) We deepen our understanding and practice of the Catholic faith throughout life. Every stage presents new opportunities and challenges. (3) We live and grow in community. Vatican

II emphasized that the Catholic faith needed to become more personal and more communal at the same time.

Inspired by the Council, the church embraced a dynamic view of catechesis. The goal has become an active, living discipleship and a personal relationship with Jesus Christ. This goes far beyond the minimalist approach prior to Vatican II. Faith formation combines *informing* people by nurturing their minds and hearts in the wisdom of the Catholic faith so that who they are and how they live are deeply influenced by what they "know," *forming* people by nurturing their identity and lifestyle in Christian discipleship, and *transforming* people by empowering them to live their faith so that the world is transformed by the Catholic vision.

Looking Ahead

What are the implications of this renewed vision of faith formation? How can we create supportive faith communities for the Catholic way of life at home and in the parish? How can we learn and live our Catholic faith today? Here are three suggestions that each of us can act on individually, within our families and together with the leaders of our parish communities.

Embrace Lifelong Learning

Over the past twenty-five years we have become a society of lifelong learners. At many American universities, the largest program is the school of continuing education. Twenty years ago Elderhostel was a small program; today it is an international program involving millions of older adults in a wide variety of learning activities. Think of all the ways that you continue learning for your job or for personal enrichment.

We need to become a church of lifelong learners. Vatican II challenged each of us to take responsibility for our own faith growth and learning. And the good news is that there has been an explosion of programs and resources to nurture our continued faith growth: adult education programs, small faith-sharing groups, Bible studies, books, video and audio programs and online learning.

Deepening our understanding and practice of the Catholic faith needs to be a top priority for us all. Learning how to apply our faith to the issues and problems of our world today is an urgent challenge for every Catholic. The static view of faith and learning is dead.

The Second Vatican Council and the catechetical documents produced since have challenged parish communities to provide lifelong faith formation, a vision still not fully realized. We need to encourage our parish communities to provide resources, programs, small groups and activities to nurture faith growth from birth through the later years of life.

One of the most hopeful signs in lifelong faith formation is the introduction of intergenerational learning programs that gather all ages in the parish to learn, pray, celebrate and share together. Intergenerational learning builds community and meaningful relationships across all the generations in a parish, provides a setting for each generation to share and learn from the other generations (their faith, stories, wisdom, experience and knowledge), creates an environment in which new ways of living one's faith can be practiced and provides adult role models for children and youth.

Become Active in a Learning Community—Your Parish
We often think of education as a teacher instructing students, a "top-down" model in which one person has the information a group of people needs. A new understanding of learning sees the role of the entire community. In a true learning community, everyone is actively engaged in learning and in teaching.

Consider the learning opportunities in the life and people of your parish. Every year the church offers a fifty-two-week learning program: the church year. We hear the story of Jesus through the lectionary, Sunday Mass and the cycle of seasons and feasts. Are we tuned into the church year so that it can inform, form and transform us?

When we immerse ourselves in the church year we journey with Jesus on the road of discipleship; we grow in intimacy and communion with him. Why not gather pilgrims to share this journey? Find time each week for reflection and discussion. In addition to the Scriptures, there are many terrific resources to guide you on the journey. This is only one way that the parish can become your learning community.

Parish leaders need to take seriously the implications of the parish as a learning community. Parishes need to provide learning opportunities that prepare people for active, conscious, meaningful participation in the church year, sacraments and works of justice and service. Parishes also need to help people reflect on their learning.

Share Faith at Home

Vatican II and subsequent teachings by Pope John Paul II and the U.S. bishops all emphasize the importance of the family in faith formation. In *Follow the Way of Love*, the U.S. bishops remind us, "A family is our first community and the most basic way in which the Lord gathers us, forms us and acts in the world. The point of the teaching is simple, yet profound. As Christian families you not only belong to the church, but your daily life is a true expression of the church."

We need to re-create a pattern of family faith sharing by learning about the Catholic faith at home, praying together, celebrating rituals, enriching family relationships and serving the needy. Start simply by finding a time each day (at a meal or end of the day) to read the daily Gospel and pray a short prayer as a family.

During the Advent-Christmas and Lent-Easter seasons, introduce special family traditions such as table prayers for the season, blessings for special meals, an Advent wreath, a day-by-day calendar of activities or a seasonal service project. Celebrate special rituals for birthdays, anniversaries and family accomplishments. Use some of your vacation time for a family service project. With each new tradition, you will slowly build a pattern of family faith sharing.

Parishes have an important role in supporting families in their faith-sharing efforts by teaching the skills for family faith sharing, modeling or demonstrating the types of activities we want families to incorporate into daily living and providing resources for home faith sharing. Parishes need to equip and empower family members, especially parents, for this important task.

CHALLENGES FOR THE FUTURE

We live in times that present new challenges for developing a Catholic way of life and sharing our faith with the next generation. We come to this task with the wisdom learned over the past forty years from the pioneers of the renewal of faith formation in the church. We come to this task with an abundance of resources for parish and home faith formation. We come to this task with the energy and enthusiasm that are the gifts of the Holy Spirit. In *The Church in the Modern World* the Council Fathers remind us that "the future of humanity lies in the hands of those who are strong enough to provide coming generations with reasons for living and hoping" (32). May we rise to the challenge.

GETTING PERSONAL
CATHERINE PINKERTON, C.S.J.

Like most young women choosing religious life years ago, Sister Catherine Pinkerton expected to spend most of her days in the classroom. And she did for a time. But when the Cleveland native entered the Sisters of St. Joseph sixty-five years ago, she didn't have an inkling of the changes that would come and the new world that would be opened to her and other women in religious life through the Second Vatican Council.

With the Council, "a church that hadn't existed came into existence," Sister Catherine said. It's a church she was more than ready for. As a young postulant she had been "frustrated with

our lack of involvement in the world." She wondered if religious life was going to work for her
and clung to her superior's assurance that "something will make us change."

That change came through Vatican II with its
focus on justice and appreciation of the contribution of women religious as well as the new sisters'
formation groups that formed before and after
the Council.

Her own life took new directions, including
congregational and national leadership. For the
past twenty years she has worked as a lobbyist on
Capitol Hill for Network, the Catholic social-jus-
tice lobby. Issues she has focused on include trade
and investments, Medicare, family farms and glob-
alization.

Like the founding members of her community in Le Pui, France, three hundred fifty years
ago, Sister Catherine, now eighty-three, believes
that women religious are called to be in the world,
not apart from it. "It's not enough to preach the
gospel. We should stand on the prophetic margins
of the church."

A NEW LANGUAGE

family catechesis: the intentional sharing of faith
and explanation of the religious meaning of
events and actions among family members of all
ages. "Family catechesis precedes...accompanies
and enriches all forms of catechesis" (*General
Directory for Catechesis,* 226).

faith formation: a term often used more or less
interchangeably with *catechesis, religious education*
and *Christian education.* When used in distinction
to these terms, its meaning includes everything

that contributes to a person's growth in communion and intimacy with Jesus Christ. This includes evangelization, intentional religious instruction, liturgy, faith sharing and personal prayer as well as life experiences.

Questions for Discussion and Reflection

• Which of the changes mentioned in this chapter have you experienced in your own lifetime? How have you responded to these changes?

• How well is your parish providing opportunities for lifelong faith formation and serving as a learning community for all of its members? What more can be done?

• How can you become more of a lifelong learner in terms of your Catholic faith?

CHAPTER TWELVE
Jesus Christ: The Model for All Humanity
JACK WINTZ, O.F.M.

For Christians, the importance of being a disciple of Jesus is quite obvious. Jesus is our source of life and salvation. Scripture passages attesting to this readily come to mind. Peter says of Jesus, for example, "There is salvation for no one else, for there is no other name under heaven given among mortals by which we must be saved" (Acts 4:12).

> The belief that Christ is the model for all humanity...gives a deep and illuminating answer to the question of why we should be imitators and disciples of Christ.

The Second Vatican Council, too, reminds us what we already know: that Jesus won salvation for us "by his blood which he freely shed" (*Pastoral Constitution on the Church in the Modern World, Gaudium et Spes*, 22) and "sent the apostles into the whole world, commanding them: 'Go, therefore, and make disciples of all nations, baptizing them in the name of the Father, and of the Son and of the Holy Spirit'" (*Decree on the Church's Missionary Activity*, 5). Each of us who has become a disciple of Christ and member of the church through baptism is called to play a part in the saving mission of Christ and the church.

Beyond these familiar truths, Vatican II also takes us to new ground in our understanding of discipleship. Especially in its *Pastoral Constitution on the Church in the Modern World*, we are introduced to the engaging idea of Christ as the model for all humanity. It's not only baptized Christians who are to find meaning in embracing Christ as a model. The Council invites the rest of the human family to do the same, to see Christ as one who will invest humanity with great meaning and dignity. Throughout this document, the bishops see themselves as "bearers of a message of salvation for all of humanity" (*Gaudium et Spes*, 1). They want to address not only the members of their own flock, "but the whole of humanity as well" (*Gaudium et Spes*, 2). The church leaders do not see themselves as separated from the larger human family whose struggles they share.

Nothing says this so well as the powerful opening lines of this groundbreaking document: "The joys and hopes, the grief and anguish of the people of our time...are the joys and hopes, the grief and anguish of the followers of Christ as well. Nothing that is genuinely human fails to find an echo in their hearts....That is why they cherish a feeling of deep solidarity with the human race and its history" (*Gaudium et Spes,* 1).

THEN AND NOW
LATERAN I (1123)

If the printing press had existed when the First Lateran Council met, the headline could have been prepared in advance: Church Council Ratifies Concordat of Worms.

It was clear from the start what the bishops and abbots who gathered for the Council in Rome in April 1123 would do: They would affirm the agreement Pope Callistus II had reached the year before with the German emperor at Worms ending the emperor's right to appoint and install bishops and abbots. That right, officially called investiture, was restored to the church after fifty or so years of struggle. The Concordat and Lateran I thus helped clarify the spiritual authority of the church in the selection of its leaders and ended state interference in papal elections. In turn, the church conceded that lay rulers could be present for the elections of bishops and abbots.

The three hundred bishops and six hundred abbots who participated in Lateran I for a mere twenty-three days helped restore a measure of peace and discipline to the church. They tackled other reforms, not all of them consequential.

These included the ruling that anyone who intentionally spent counterfeit money would be separated from the church and viewed as an oppressor of the poor.

CHRIST: THE PERFECT HUMAN

The belief that Christ is the model for all humanity is a signature teaching of Vatican II that gives a deep and illuminating answer to the question of why we should be imitators and disciples of Christ. As the Council states, "The church...believes that the key, the center and the purpose of the whole of human history, is to be found in its Lord and Master" (*Gaudium et Spes*, 10). The Council later affirms, "It is only in the mystery of the Word made flesh that the mystery of humanity truly becomes clear...Christ, in the very revelation of the mystery of the Father and his love, *fully reveals humanity to itself* and brings to light its very high calling" (*Gaudium et Spes*, 22; emphasis added).

As one becomes a disciple and imitator of Christ, the document implies, one does not abandon one's humanity or become less human. Rather, one becomes more fully human. "To follow Christ, the perfect human," the Council states, "is to become more human oneself" (*Gaudium et Spes*, 41).

The Council sums up its teaching on Christ as the key to understanding the meaning and destiny of humanity in these words: "The Lord is the goal of human history, the focal point of the desires of history and civilization, the center of humanity, the joy of all hearts and the fulfillment of all aspirations.... Animated and drawn together in his Spirit, we press onwards on our journey towards the consummation of history which fully corresponds to the plan of his love: 'to unite all things in him, things in heaven and things on earth' (Eph 1:10)" (*Gaudium et Spes*, 45).

GETTING PERSONAL
BISHOP IGNATIUS WANG

Growing up in Beijing, China, in the 1930s and 1940s, young Ignatius Wang and his family lived in an almost exclusively Catholic neighborhood. Saturday afternoon confession and Sunday morning Mass were weekend rituals. Vatican II and its document on religious liberty were still years away.

For China, the dark days came with the arrival of the Cultural Revolution (1965–1975). It was then that "most churches, synagogues and temples were destroyed or converted into other uses," now-Bishop Wang said. He had already left home by then, first for seminary studies in Hong Kong, then on to Rome and Grenada. He now serves as auxiliary bishop of San Francisco.

Today the Chinese constitution guarantees religious freedom, but "is often interpreted differently at various levels and places. Religious freedom is not really encouraged because communism, per se, proclaims atheism," Bishop Wang explains. The government-controlled Chinese Bishops' Conference names new bishops "with or without Vatican approval." But on a practical basis, Bishop Wang says, "The people don't worry about it as long as they can go to church freely."

"Religious liberty is most precarious for so-called 'underground Catholics,' who remain loyal to Rome and who are at risk of arrest," he said. Still, their "unregistered churches often operate freely; some openly display crosses on their roofs. The situation varies from place to place."

The church in China still has its struggles, but it is "catching up to the teaching of Vatican II," and its "spirit of evangelization appeals to the present generation."

POPE JOHN PAUL II ADVANCES THIS TEACHING

During his years as bishop and archbishop of Krakow, Karol Wojtyla—who became Pope John Paul II—attended all four sessions of Vatican II (1962–1965) and served on several important committees. When he was elected pope in 1978, he saw it as his duty to continue the implementation of the Council.

One Council teaching that he especially took to heart was this notion of Christ as the "goal of human history" and the model for all of humanity. The first line of his first encyclical, *The Redeemer of the Human Race,* is "Christ is the center of the universe and of human history." Several of the ideas and passages quoted above from Vatican II's *Pastoral Constitution on the Church in the Modern World* found their way into his encyclical.

In addition, the idea that Christ is the model and key for understanding the full meaning of our humanity also began surfacing in his speeches around the world. For example, during his first trip to Poland as pope in June 1979, John Paul II gave a bold and dramatic address to Catholics gathered in Warsaw's Victory Square where a good number of the Communist Party leaders were also in attendance. "To Poland," the pope proclaimed, "the church brought Christ, the key to understanding the great and fundamental reality that is man." And because of this, the pope continued, "Christ cannot be excluded from human history in any part of the globe, from any latitude or longitude of the earth. Excluding Christ from human history is a sin against humanity."

Pope John Paul II brought a similar message to American youth at New York's Madison Square Garden on October 3 of the same year: "When you wonder about the mystery of yourself, look to Christ who gives you the meaning of life. When you wonder what it means to be a mature person, look to Christ who is the fullness of humanity."

FIVE WAYS TO BE A DISCIPLE TODAY

Reflection on the documents of the Second Vatican Council has led me to compile the following list of significant characteristics of today's disciples.

Today's disciples are servants of humanity. The documents of Vatican II encouraged church members to place themselves in solidarity with the struggles and aspirations of the whole human family. In his first visit to the United States as pope in October of 1979, John Paul II expressed exactly this attitude. To an immense and diverse crowd in Boston, the first stop of his journey, the pope said, "I want to greet all Americans without distinction. I want to tell you that the pope is your friend and a servant of your humanity."

Indeed, the spirit of the Council led its followers to see themselves as servants of the human race and supporters of the positive signs of authentic human progress—even when discovered outside the borders of the church. True disciples, the Council taught, should avoid thinking that "what human enterprise and ability have achieved is…a rival to the creator." Rather, it says, "Christians are convinced that the achievements of the human race are a sign of God's greatness and the fulfillment of his mysterious design" (*Gaudium et Spes,* 34).

Today's disciples seek vital union with the risen Christ. This union is fostered through prayer. But it happens especially in the context of the Eucharist and the sacraments of the church, as revitalized by the liturgical reforms of Vatican II. Most notable among these reforms has been the "full, conscious and active" participation in liturgical celebrations on the part of all the faithful (*Constitution on the Sacred Liturgy, Sacrosanctum Concilium,* 14).

We encounter the risen Jesus most fruitfully in the sacraments. "By baptism," the *Constitution on the Sacred Liturgy* tells us, "men and women are implanted in the paschal mystery of Christ; they die with him, are buried with him and rise with him"—becoming children of God (6).

It is especially in the Eucharist, "the source and summit of the Christian life" (*Dogmatic Constitution on the Church,* 11), that disciples of Christ place themselves in intimate union with the risen Christ. It was in the context of the Last Supper, we may recall, that Jesus advised his first disciples, "Abide in me, as I abide in you" (John 15:4). He used the image of a branch remaining on the vine to convey the utter intimacy of this union—an image that disciples of our era need to keep pondering.

Today's disciples show special concern for the poor. Even though human progress has benefited many, almost every society has great numbers of people who are severely disadvantaged and needy. Socially aware followers of Christ in our day look for ways to reach out to those who are poor and "the least of Jesus' brothers and sisters" (see Matthew 25:40). Some individual Christians and parish communities make generous efforts to provide food for the hungry and shelter for the homeless and, perhaps even better, seek to change unjust social structures and laws in order to set free the oppressed. This, too, is a vital part of our mission as followers of Jesus today.

Today's disciples struggle to build a more peaceful and united world. Men and women who work to overcome the divisions separating Christian churches are certainly among the peacemakers praised and described by Christ as "children of God" (Matthew 5:9). So also are those who strive patiently to create a better atmosphere of love and understanding between Christians and members of other world religions such as Islam and Judaism. In light of Vatican II's *Decree on Ecumenism* and *Declaration on the Relation of the Church to Non-Christian Religions,* all those engaged in the noble task of removing walls and promoting the unity of the human family should be viewed as truly performing part of Jesus' mission in our time.

Today's disciples take a broad and optimistic view of God's saving love. Vatican II holds up to us the image of a gracious "God who 'wills that all be saved and come to the knowledge of the truth' (1 Tim 2:4)" (*Constitution on the Sacred Liturgy,* 5). Yes, the Council assures Christians that they are saved through Jesus' life, death and resurrection. But the Council also states: "All this holds true not only for Christians but also for all people of good will in whose hearts grace is active invisibly. For since Christ died for everyone, and since all are in fact called to one and the same destiny, which is divine, we must hold that the Holy Spirit offers to all the possibility of being made partners, in a way known to God, in the paschal mystery" (*Gaudium et Spes,* 22). The follower of Christ, therefore, does not hesitate to work confidently and hopefully in partnership with the whole human family.

Our lives and church have changed in so many ways since the Second Vatican Council ended in December of 1965. God's love and the Spirit's guidance remain constants through times of change. One way the Spirit guides Christian disciples is through the documents of the Council. As we continue to grow in our understanding of the vision of Vatican II, may each of us also grow into the fullness of our humanity and strive to live as true disciples of Christ.

A NEW LANGUAGE

church as mystery: the church is more than a human reality; it was divinely founded and continues to be guided by the Holy Spirit. We don't have all of the answers but we are searching for the truth.

church as sacrament: the Body of Christ, all of Christianity, which makes God present to the world; the Christian church is the "universal sacrament of salvation" (*Dogmatic Constitution on the Church,* 48).

church as pilgrim: an incomplete and imperfect community that continues to change and journey toward the fullness of truth, who is God.

Questions for Discussion and Reflection

• What do you make of the statement that Jesus is the model for all humanity? How does your Christian discipleship invite you to become more fully human?

• How well are you living the five characteristics of a disciple listed in this chapter? To which one(s) do you need to give more attention?

• What more must you do to continue to grow in your understanding of the vision of Vatican II and into the fullness of your humanity as a true disciple of Christ?

THE DOCUMENTS OF VATICAN II

Ad Gentes, "Decree on the Missionary Activity of the Church"
The Church, by its very nature, is missionary—it proclaims the message of Jesus the Christ to all humanity. Stresses that missionaries must be respectful of the cultures in which they share the person of Jesus.

Apostolicam Actuositatem, "Decree on the Apostolate of the Laity"
Lay faithful, as a result of their baptisms, are called to be leaven in the world. Not only do the laity have charisms to offer the Church, but, more importantly, they have gifts to share in the temporal order—family, culture, economics, arts, professions and politics.

Christus Dominus, "Decree on the Bishops' Pastoral Office in the Church"
Speaks of the rights and responsibilities of bishops both in union with the pope and as applied to their particular dioceses. Revived the ancient practice of episcopal conferences.

Dei Verbum, "Dogmatic Constitution on Divine Revelation"
Jesus is the mediator and fullness of God's revelation. The Word of God is revealed both in scripture and tradition. The teaching office of the Church—the magisterium—is entrusted with the task of authentically interpreting the Word of God.

Dignitatis Humanae, "Declaration on Religious Freedom"
Argues that in virtue of one's humanity, all have the right to live according to their conscience in the exercise of their religious beliefs. Church seeks to persuade believers, never coerce. Its acceptance hinged on the admittance of doctrinal development.

Gaudium et Spes, "Pastoral Constitution on the Church in the Modern World"
The Church must respond to the signs of the times: the joys and the hopes, the griefs and anxieties of the people of the world are shared by the Church. It offers itself in service to the whole of humanity.

Gravissimum Educationis, "Declaration on Christian Education"
Education, as the formation of the whole person, is a human right not a privilege. With respect to religious education, parents are seen as the primary educators in faith. Catholic schools and colleges are mentioned as important places where faith formation takes place.

Inter Mirifica, "Decree on the Means of Social Communication"
Recognizes the great potential (and possible abuse) of media forms:

newspapers, movies, radio, and television. Sees the media as a means to communicate the Gospel.

Lumen Gentium, "Dogmatic Constitution on the Church"
Envisions the Church as a sign and sacrament of God. Speaks of the hierarchy as serving the entire Church, the People of God. Calls the whole Church, rather than just the ordained, to a life of holiness.

Nostra Aetate, "Declaration on the Relationship of the Church to Non-Christian Religions"
Revolutionizes the Church's relationship with other world religions, especially Judaism, by admitting that they too possess truth and holiness. Repudiates anti-Semitism and the notion that Jews are guilty for the death of Jesus.

Optatam Totius, "Decree on Priestly Formation"
Revises seminary training, highlighting that students need to be grounded in the Word of God (Scripture), worship, and pastoral ministry. Promotes continued learning for those already ordained.

Orientalium Ecclesiarum, "Decree on the Catholic Eastern Churches"
Expresses value and a desire for the renewal of the institutions, liturgy, and traditions of the Eastern Catholic churches.

Perfectae Caritatis, "Decree on the Renewal of Religious Life"
Asks that religious return to the charism of their founder, and, when appropriate, adapt to the changing culture of the day.

Presbyterorum Ordinis, "Decree on the Ministry and Life of Priests"
Mindful of the changing culture, the priest is charged with leading people to Christ. This is to be done through the priest's own witness and the celebration of the sacraments, chiefly the Eucharist.

Sacrosanctum Concilium, "Constitution on the Sacred Liturgy"
Seeks to encourage and bring about full, conscious and active participation in the liturgy. Open to change in regard to nonessentials which leads to the re-introduction of the vernacular. Arguably, the one document which most touches Catholics in the pews.

Unitatis Redintegratio, "Decree on Ecumenism"
Desires the restoration of union, not simply a return to Rome, among all Christians. Admits that both sides were to blame for historical divisions. Gives guidelines for the practice of church union.

INDEX